AF797115

PAT BROWN, MBA

Financial Literacy For Teachers

"Smart Money Lessons for Educators Who Want to Build Wealth and Peace of Mind."

ABRAM · 47 · BROWN

First published by AbramBrown47 2025

Copyright © 2025 by Pat Brown, MBA

All rights reserved. No part of this publication may be reproduced, stored or transmitted in any form or by any means, electronic, mechanical, photocopying, recording, scanning, or otherwise without written permission from the publisher. It is illegal to copy this book, post it to a website, or distribute it by any other means without permission.

Pat Brown, MBA asserts the moral right to be identified as the author of this work.

Pat Brown, MBA has no responsibility for the persistence or accuracy of URLs for external or third-party Internet Websites referred to in this publication and does not guarantee that any content on such Websites is, or will remain, accurate or appropriate.

Designations used by companies to distinguish their products are often claimed as trademarks. All brand names and product names used in this book and on its cover are trade names, service marks, trademarks and registered trademarks of their respective owners. The publishers and the book are not associated with any product or vendor mentioned in this book. None of the companies referenced within the book have endorsed the book.

First edition

ISBN: 978-1-967737-43-7

This book was professionally typeset on Reedsy.
Find out more at reedsy.com

Contents

Preface

I've had the privilege of sitting across the table from countless clients over the years—professionals of all kinds—but the teachers? They hold a special place. Many of my clients are educators, and I can say without hesitation that teachers are some of the most dedicated, selfless, and quietly heroic individuals I've ever worked with. They give more than they're asked to. They carry more than they're paid for. And they are called to do more than they're often credited for.

That's why I wrote this book.

Financial Literacy for Teachers was born out of those one-on-one conversations I've had with educators—those moments where the numbers didn't make sense, the retirement options were confusing, the paycheck didn't stretch far enough, and yet... the work never stopped. I saw brilliant, capable professionals who could manage 30 kids, adapt to shifting curriculum standards, and navigate parent meetings with grace—but who had never been taught how to fully understand their own financial lives. Not because they weren't intelligent, but because no one ever showed them how the financial system works in a way that made sense *for them.*

This book is my response to that gap. It's a guide. It's a resource. But more than that—it's a recognition. A recognition that teaching is a calling, and that answering that call often comes with emotional rewards and financial strain. Teachers are told to be mentors, counselors, curriculum designers, disciplinarians, advocates, and cheerleaders—all while managing rising costs of living, supporting families, and funding their classrooms out of their own pockets.

I've worked with teachers who are just starting out—excited to sign their first contract, but overwhelmed by their benefits packet and unsure how to manage student loan payments. I've worked with mid-career educators who are raising children, caring for aging parents, and wondering how they'll ever catch up financially. I've walked with retiring teachers who've spent thirty years giving everything to their students, but now aren't sure if their pension will be enough to support the retirement they deserve.

This book is written for all of them—and for you.

It's not about finger-wagging or guilt. It's not a "stop-buying-coffee" manifesto. It's about teaching the foundational truths that too many teachers were never taught: how credit works, how pensions are calculated, how to use a 403(b) or 457, how to decide between renting or buying, how to build a financial plan when you're a single teacher with kids or a married couple working in the same district. It's about breaking down big ideas—like investing, taxes, insurance, estate planning—and translating them into action that actually fits a teacher's life.

I want you to feel seen on every page. Whether you're in your 20s or your 60s, whether you teach kindergarten or AP calculus, whether you're burned out or just starting to build momentum—this book was written with your reality in mind. It respects the emotional labor of your work. It understands the financial limitations of your paycheck. And it doesn't treat you like someone who needs a crash course in budgeting. You don't need to be told to "just save more." You need clarity. Tools. Strategy. Confidence. You need someone who speaks your language and respects your time.

Throughout this book, you'll find chapters that dig deep into the financial decisions that define the life of an educator—buying your first home, protecting your income with insurance, setting up a legacy through estate planning, choosing when and how to retire. You'll also find perspectives on family life—how to support your kids financially, how to talk to them about money, how to care for your parents while still preparing for your own future. We'll even explore what it looks like to have conversations with your students about financial literacy when age-appropriate, and how to bring other educators into this journey—perhaps even through a teacher financial book club.

Importantly, every chapter ends differently. There are no repeated slogans or scripted closings. Life isn't one-size-fits-all, and this book respects that. Some chapters will end with action steps. Others with insight. Some may leave you with a tough truth to reflect on. But none of them will talk down to you. None will wrap up your challenges in a bow. This book is real—because your life is real.

You didn't enter this profession to get rich. But that doesn't mean you should settle for being financially stuck, stressed, or silent. You can be a phenomenal teacher *and* a financially secure one. You can care for your students *and* care for your future. You can build a legacy—not just in the classroom, but in your bank account, your estate plan, your family, and your peace of mind.

I believe in you. I believe in the power of teachers. And I believe it's time the financial world started believing in you, too.

Welcome to *Financial Literacy for Teachers.*

Pat Brown, MBA

Financial Literacy Advocate | Wealth Manager

You Didn't Become a Teacher to Be Rich—But That Doesn't Mean You Should Stay Broke

If you're holding this book, it means you already understand something that many people never take the time to realize: real wealth isn't just about how much you earn. It's not just about a pension formula, a Roth IRA balance, or whether you qualify for loan forgiveness. Wealth—real, grounded, lasting wealth—isn't about a number on a statement. It's about something far more powerful.

It's about **control**—over your time, your options, your future.

It's about **stewardship**—over your energy, your resources, and your legacy.

And above all, it's about **responsibility**—to yourself, your loved ones, and the life you want to build.

You didn't choose teaching for the paycheck. You chose it because you believe in impact, in learning, in shaping the next generation. But that doesn't mean you should be financially stressed for the rest of your life. You deserve to live with clarity and confidence around your money. You deserve peace—not just summers off, but year-round peace of mind.

In my work with teachers across the country, I've heard the same quiet frustrations again and again: "I wish someone had taught me this sooner." "I didn't realize I had more than one retirement option." "I didn't know how my pension actually worked until it was almost too late." "I'm embarrassed that I've been teaching personal responsibility for twenty years and don't feel in control of my own finances." If any of that sounds familiar, you're not alone—and you're not behind. You've simply never had a guide built for you.

That's what this book is.

Not a lecture. Not a guilt trip. Not a collection of money hacks designed for people in a totally different tax bracket or lifestyle. This is a straight-talking, judgment-free roadmap to financial literacy—for educators, by someone who's worked with hundreds of them, and who understands the reality of your world.

We'll talk about everything from student loans to 403(b)s, from budgeting that actually fits your teaching life to insurance, estate planning, and side income. We'll look at how to plan for your children's future without sacrificing your own. We'll talk about pensions, Roth IRAs, tax strategies for two-teacher households, and why your paycheck doesn't tell the full story. And yes—we'll get honest about what to do when you're tired, underpaid, and wondering if it's even worth trying.

Because here's the truth: teaching is a calling, but financial wellness is a skill—and it can be learned.

You don't need to become a financial expert. You just need to learn how to think about your money with confidence and make decisions that work for *you*. You already help students make sense of the world. Now it's time to help yourself make sense of your finances—without shame, without fear, and without waiting another year.

This is your classroom now. Let's get started.

—Pat Brown, MBA

Financial Educator | Wealth Advisor | Advocate for Teachers' Financial Peace

A Note on Wealth: Why This Isn't Just About Money

The world often sees wealth—whether in the form of a large pension, a modest investment account, or a home finally paid off—and assumes ease. It assumes security. It assumes a finish line has been crossed. But if you're a teacher reading this, you already know the truth: real financial peace doesn't come from a number in your bank account. It comes from understanding, from clarity, and from having a plan you can trust.

Financial complexity doesn't disappear just because you've spent 30 years in a classroom. It often intensifies. Pension rules. Health insurance in retirement. Student loan forgiveness. Helping aging parents. Supporting adult kids. Managing credit. Navigating investments. These aren't textbook problems with multiple choice answers. These are real-life pressures, and many teachers face them silently—because the outside world rarely understands how heavy it can all feel.

When you shift from trying to get by month-to-month to trying to secure the next 20 or 30 years, the work gets harder—not easier. You're not just budgeting for the summer anymore. You're thinking about long-term care. About Medicare. About inflation. About whether your benefits will keep pace with the cost of living. And you're doing all of this while still grading papers, mentoring new teachers, and carrying the emotional load of your classroom.

For many teachers, the transition from simplicity to complexity happens quietly. You go from wondering how to pay off loans to wondering how to help your kids through college. From living paycheck to paycheck to wondering if your investments are too conservative—or too aggressive. You might have options now, but those options come with more decisions, and more at stake.

That's where clarity comes in.

This isn't about mastering Wall Street. It's about mastering *your* street. Your pension. Your healthcare choices. Your retirement income. Your insurance coverage. Your tax planning. Your will. Your home. It's about simplifying the complex in a way that doesn't leave you feeling like you missed a class everyone else took.

And yes—money can bring freedom. But it can also bring isolation if you're the only one in your circle who understands these decisions. If you're the one explaining to your family why you're not co-signing a loan or why you can't afford to take on everyone else's problems just because you "have a pension."

This book won't just walk you through financial facts. It will ask you to think critically about boundaries, values, and what kind of life you want your money to support. It will show you that wealth isn't always about having more—it's about using what you have wisely and protecting your peace along the way.

Your role as a teacher has always been about building futures. This is your moment to build your own—intentionally, confidently, and without shame.

If there's one challenge I'd give you right now, it's this:

Pick one area of your financial life that feels unresolved—retirement planning, credit management, legacy planning, insurance, helping your kids, or helping your parents. Write it down. Be honest about what's unclear, or what's weighing on you.

Then do one thing this week to move forward. It could be small. Call your benefits office. Open a Roth IRA. Read your pension estimate. Have a family conversation about money. Ask a professional a question you've been too afraid to ask.

One move. This week.

Because peace of mind isn't built in a day. But it *is* built.

You've educated generations. Now it's your turn to master your money—on your terms, with your values, and with a voice that's finally being heard.

You're not late. You're just getting started.

How to Use This Book

This book wasn't built to be read in one sitting.

It was built to be used — as a guide, a reference, and a companion for the financial decisions you face as a teacher, both in and out of the classroom.

Whether you're in your first year of teaching or approaching retirement, your financial questions are real, personal, and time-sensitive. That's why this book is designed to meet you where you are — not where someone else thinks you *should* be.

You can read this book front to back. But you don't have to. In fact, you probably shouldn't. Here's how to get the most out of it:

1. Start With What Matters Most to You Right Now

Skim the table of contents. See what jumps out.

Are you trying to make a tight paycheck stretch through the summer? Are you worried about student loans or wondering if your district's retirement plan is enough? Do you need help understanding your health insurance options?

Start there. You don't need to be "financially ready" to dig in — you just need to be honest about what's keeping you up at night.

2. Use Each Chapter as a Standalone Resource

Every chapter in this book is structured to stand on its own. You'll find clear explanations, common-sense comparisons, relatable teacher examples, and practical next steps.

You can read one chapter this week, come back to a different chapter next month, and still move forward.

This is not theory — this is everyday reality, broken down with respect for your time, your profession, and your paycheck.

3. Don't Worry About Getting It Perfect

You don't need a financial background. You don't need to understand every acronym. And you don't need to make every financial move at once.

What matters most is progress — not perfection.

This book will walk you through decisions in plain language, with tools you can use in real life: checklists, questions to ask HR, pros and cons of different options, and actions you can take as soon as today.

4. Come Back Often

Your career evolves. Your salary changes. Your family grows. Life happens.

Come back to this book at every new stage — whether you're switching districts, getting married, preparing to send your own kids to college, or planning your retirement.

What didn't feel relevant last year might be essential today.

Think of this book like your lesson plan binder: it's always there when you need it, and it gets more useful over time.

5. Use It With Your Spouse, Colleagues, or Financial Advisor

Financial literacy is personal, but it doesn't have to be private.

If your spouse is also a teacher, read chapters together. If your friends are asking the same money questions you are, share what you've learned.

And if you have a financial advisor, use this book as a conversation starter — so *you* can be the one asking the smart questions.

6. Act As You Go

Every chapter closes with one or more action steps — specific things you can do this week, this month, or this school year. These aren't vague goals — they're real moves that build clarity, confidence, and control.

Whether it's opening a Roth IRA, rethinking how you handle summer pay, or finally understanding your pension, one small step can shift your entire mindset.

7. Come With Questions — Not Shame

There is no shame in not knowing.

Nobody taught you this in undergrad. Nobody trained you on this during student teaching. And nobody should expect you to master retirement plans, tax codes, insurance options, and debt strategies without help.

This book exists because you deserve help. You deserve answers. You deserve options.

Final Note:

This book isn't just about money.

It's about peace of mind.

It's about stability.

It's about knowing that you can care for others *and* take care of yourself.

You already teach the world.

Now it's time to own your financial story — and shape the life you want with the paycheck you have.

The Problem With Traditional Advice (And Why Teachers Deserve Better)

If you've ever sat across from a traditional financial advisor as a teacher, you've probably felt it — that moment when their recommendations seem disconnected from your reality. It's not personal. The truth is, much of the financial advice in this country is built on assumptions. Assumptions about income levels. Assumptions about career paths. Assumptions about priorities. And most of all, assumptions that don't reflect the unique financial lives of educators.

You work in one of the most essential, underappreciated professions in society — yet so much of the wealth management industry was not built with you in mind. The advice is often geared toward executives, entrepreneurs, or high-earning professionals with stock options, bonuses, and corporate retirement perks. But what about teachers who are navigating pension systems, second jobs, student loans, irregular pay cycles, and the decision to support aging parents or help their own children through college?

You deserve better. Not just more respect — but better strategies. Because financial advice should match the life you actually live.

One-Size-Fits-All Doesn't Fit a Classroom Career

Most personal finance tools out there rely on generic formulas: the "50/30/20" budgeting rule, standard retirement contribution advice, or quick calculators that assume everyone has access to the same benefits. But that's not the case in education. Teachers face unique variables — like pension eligibility, state-specific retirement systems, optional 403(b) or 457 plans, and pay structures that fluctuate depending on contract length and district policies.

Those tools might work fine for a tech worker in a private sector job. But they fall apart when applied to a teacher trying to budget through the summer, plan for retirement while raising kids, or determine whether to buy a home on a modest salary in a high-cost-of-living area.

What you need isn't another generic budget sheet or investment tip. You need guidance that reflects your profession — your income, your goals, your constraints, and your values.

Most Advisors Don't Understand Teacher Pay and Benefits

Let's be honest: most financial advisors haven't taken the time to understand the inner workings of teacher pensions, step raises, contract negotiations, or the emotional pull to "give back" even when your paycheck doesn't stretch far enough.

They may understand 401(k)s, but not the differences between a TRS plan and a 403(b). They may recommend life insurance, but fail to account for the group coverage you already have through your district. They may push Roth IRAs without asking how your state's pension affects your taxable income later in life.

It's not that they don't care — it's that their training rarely includes a deep dive into the lives of public servants. You deserve advice that starts with listening — and ends with solutions designed around your actual choices and tradeoffs.

Simplicity That Actually Works

One myth that persists is that financial literacy needs to be complex to be meaningful. That's not true. Good financial planning should feel like a clear, steady conversation — not a maze of jargon and charts.

Real sophistication comes from clarity, not confusion.

When your financial life already includes student loans, two kids, inconsistent summer pay, and a pension plan you don't fully understand, the last thing you need is more complexity. What you need is integration: clear guidance that connects your paycheck to your pension, your debt plan to your investment goals, your estate plan to your values as a parent and professional.

You Need a Financial Architect — Not a Salesperson

Think about what great teachers do: they don't hand out cookie-cutter lesson plans. They meet students where they are. They assess the room, build relationships, and adjust based on who's in front of them.

That's what a real financial advisor should do for you.

Your money plan should be *built* — not sold. It should reflect your life stage, your dreams, your fears, your trade-offs. You need someone who can ask the right questions about your district's retirement plan, help you map out the cost of helping your child through college while still taking care of your aging parent, and build a legacy — not just a budget.

Why This Matters

Teachers are leaders. You shape lives every day. But too often, your own financial life takes a back seat — to lesson planning, grading, mentoring, or putting others first.

This chapter is here to remind you: **your money matters, too.**

And when traditional advice doesn't speak your language, it's not your fault. It's because the model wasn't made for you. That's exactly why this book exists — to give you tools, not templates. A roadmap, not just a bunch of rules. Clarity, not complexity.

Pros and Cons of Personalized Financial Planning for Educators

Pros:

- Custom strategies built around your pay cycle, benefits, and pension plan.

- Guidance that connects retirement, insurance, budgeting, and family needs.
- Confidence to make informed decisions without second-guessing.
- A support system that values your profession and your time.

Cons:

- Not all advisors are qualified to help teachers — choose wisely.
- It takes effort to find someone who truly listens and understands.
- Some planning steps can feel overwhelming at first — but you don't have to do them alone.
- There may be costs involved — but the value can far outweigh the price.

Action Steps

1. **Audit your current financial setup:** Are you relying on advice that wasn't designed for you?
2. **Review your district benefits and pension options:** Do you fully understand how they impact your retirement timeline and income?
3. **Find an advisor who understands educators:** Interview more than one. Ask hard questions (there's a list in the next chapter).
4. **Pick one priority:** Maybe it's budgeting better this summer, starting a Roth IRA, or preparing for your child's college expenses.
5. **Take one step this month.** The path to financial clarity starts with movement — not mastery.

Real-Life Teacher Example

A single mother teaching middle school for 14 years was overwhelmed trying to balance saving for her daughter's college, preparing for retirement, and helping her own mother with medical expenses. She didn't need a stock-picking strategy — she needed a roadmap. By working with an advisor who specialized in educators, she created a plan to increase her 403(b) contributions, open a 529 for her daughter, and update her life insurance to reflect her current needs. She didn't do it all at once. But she started. And that changed everything.

Bottom line?

You didn't choose teaching for the money — but your money still matters.

It's time you had financial advice that respects the career you've committed your life to.

Let me know if you'd like a version of this formatted for a teacher's financial workshop or discussion guide — or if you want this broken into visual slides for your next educator event.

Teaching Isn't Just a Job — It's a Life Built on Purpose. Your Finances Should Reflect That.

If you're holding this book, you already know something most of the world tends to forget: teaching is more than a profession. It's a calling. It's a commitment to show up, give more than you take, and build futures that extend far beyond your own. But what happens when you've spent a lifetime pouring into others—and you realize no one has ever handed *you* the blueprint for building financial strength, security, and legacy?

This book is that blueprint. Not a step-by-step formula for overnight wealth, but a deep, flexible guide for educators who want more clarity, more control, and more confidence in their financial lives. If you're juggling a pension, a 403(b), student loan debt, family support obligations, a summer side hustle, and maybe even early retirement dreams—you don't need theory. You need tools that match your reality.

Building Your Financial Command Center

Many teachers manage their money in fragments: pay stubs in one drawer, retirement info in another folder, student loan statements in an inbox they avoid. But scattered systems lead to scattered thinking—and missed opportunities.

To lead your financial life with clarity, you need a centralized system. A "Teacher's Command Center" that pulls together your pay schedule, district benefits, retirement options, insurance coverage, emergency savings, student debt, and household budget in one clear view. Like a lesson plan you can trust, this system helps you lead your financial life with intention—not reaction.

Action Step: Gather your key financial documents—pay stubs, pension statements, investment accounts, loan balances—and organize them in one digital folder. Visibility is the first step toward strategy.

Creating Liquidity Without Sacrificing Your Long-Term Goals

A lot of teachers look "fine on paper," but feel stressed in real life. Your pension may sound great in theory—but you can't spend it until retirement. Your paycheck may be steady, but summer can stretch it thin. The question is: do you have flexible access to your money without derailing your long-term plans?

Liquidity is about options. It's about being able to handle an unexpected car repair, say yes to a family trip, or invest in continuing education—without draining your savings. Smart liquidity planning means building up your emergency fund, using summer savings strategies, and managing debt so that your cash flow can flex when life does.

Action Step: Do a quick liquidity check. If your paycheck stopped today, how many months could you comfortably cover your basic expenses? If the answer is less than three, it's time to prioritize building your short-term cushion.

Managing Financial Risk Like the Professional You Are

As a teacher, you may not think of yourself as someone facing "big risks." But that's a myth. You have a family depending on your income. You may be just one lawsuit, illness, or accident away from a serious setback.

Risk isn't just about market losses. It's about life happening. The real risk is being unprepared when it does.

That means having disability insurance in case you can't work. Making sure your district life insurance is enough—or getting supplemental coverage. Having an umbrella policy to protect your assets. Getting a legal will and healthcare proxy in place. You don't need to fear risk—you just need to name it, and build a plan that can absorb it.

Action Step: Schedule 30 minutes to review your insurance policies. What's covered? What's not? What's missing? Don't wait for a storm to check if you've got a roof.

Investing With Purpose, Not Pressure

Too many teachers are told they "should" be investing more—but never taught how to invest in ways that align with their values, timeline, and risk tolerance. Maybe your district offers a 403(b) or 457 plan. Maybe you've heard of Roth IRAs but aren't sure if you should open one. Maybe you've been burned by bad advice before and feel stuck.

This isn't about chasing returns. It's about building options for your future.

You don't need to be an expert. But you do need a system—one that helps you save consistently, invest wisely, and rebalance over time. Your pension may provide a foundation, but it shouldn't be the only pillar of your retirement plan.

Action Step: Log into your retirement plan portal. Look at your current investment mix. Is it too conservative? Too aggressive? Completely unclear? Ask for help if you need it. Empowered decisions start with informed eyes.

Creating a Legacy That Reflects Who You Are

You teach because you care. But when it comes to building a lasting legacy, most teachers leave it to chance. Your legacy isn't just your pension payout or your estate. It's what you model for your kids. It's how you prepare for your own aging. It's what you leave behind—not just in money, but in mindset.

Do you have a basic estate plan? A healthcare proxy? A letter to your family about your values? Are you mentoring a younger teacher on how to manage their money? Do you talk about money at the dinner table?

Action Step: Write down the top three financial lessons you want to pass on to your children, your students, or your community. You don't need millions to leave a legacy. You just need clarity and conviction.

Leading Your Own Financial Team

Most teachers are used to doing things alone. But that doesn't mean you should. Just like students need different kinds of teachers, you may need different kinds of professionals: a tax advisor, a financial planner, a mortgage broker, or even a lawyer.

The key is not just hiring someone—but building a team that works together. You don't need to be the expert in every subject. You just need to be the principal of your financial life.

Action Step: Make a list of your current financial professionals (if any). Are they talking to each other? Are they serving *your* needs—or just selling you something? Don't be afraid to ask hard questions or make changes.

Why This Matters

You've already done the hard work. You've chosen a profession rooted in service, integrity, and lifelong learning. Now it's time to build a financial life that honors that choice.

This isn't about chasing more. It's about doing better with what you've earned. About protecting what you've built. About preparing for the life you want beyond the classroom. Because whether you teach for five more years or twenty, your money should be working for *you*—not the other way around.

Choose one action step from this chapter. Just one. Do it this week.

You don't need to be perfect. You just need to start. Clarity isn't a destination—it's a discipline. And with each step, you're building not just wealth, but wisdom.

Let me know if you'd like this adapted into a workshop handout, planner section, or teacher financial checklist.

Part I: First-Year Foundations – Welcome to Teaching, Welcome to Reality

The first year of teaching is a whirlwind—new classroom, new students, new expectations, and, for many, a financial reality check that hits harder than expected. In this foundational section, we meet teachers at the beginning of their journey, where optimism meets overwhelm, and where salary numbers don't always match the emotional and physical effort required by the job.

This part is designed to walk new and early-career educators through the critical first steps of understanding how their financial lives are shaped by the structure of their job. We break down the anatomy of a teacher's paycheck, explore the often-misunderstood benefits package, and lay the groundwork for smart budgeting on a modest income. You'll learn what it really means to contribute to a pension system, how 403(b) and 457 plans work, and how to begin building credit, managing student loans, and protecting your income through the right types of insurance.

We'll also dive into the emotional side of money—how it feels to give so much to your students while struggling to afford your own essentials, and how to make peace with the challenges without settling for financial stagnation. This section is honest, direct, and empowering. It offers clarity without judgment and invites teachers to take control of their money story from day one.

Whether you're just entering the classroom or still trying to make sense of your early career finances, **Part I** sets the stage for everything to come. This is where financial literacy begins—not in the abstract, but in the lived, day-to-day experience of real teachers doing real work with limited resources and unlimited heart.

Chapter 1: Your First Paycheck – Where Did the Money Go?

You did it. You got hired. You walked into your new classroom, hopefully with your name on the door, a whiteboard full of possibilities, and a heart bursting with anticipation. And then, just a few weeks later, you received your first paycheck—and felt something very different: confusion. Maybe disappointment. Maybe frustration. Maybe even a little bit of shame. After all, you knew teachers weren't getting rich, but you also didn't expect to work this hard for this little. For many educators, that first direct deposit doesn't feel like a celebration. It feels like a riddle. Where did the money go?

Your salary looked fine on paper. You did the math in your head before signing the contract: multiply the annual salary by your pay cycle, subtract a bit for taxes, and it seemed like things would work out. But then came the deductions: federal taxes, state taxes, maybe even city taxes, and Medicare. Maybe you live in a state where you don't pay into Social Security but instead contribute to a public retirement system like TRS, STRS, or PERS. And there it is—a line on your pay stub you've never really understood but that eats a large percentage of your gross pay before it ever reaches your bank account. Add to that health insurance premiums, union dues, life insurance, long-term disability, possibly optional charitable deductions you never realized you authorized, and suddenly your "real" income is several hundred dollars less than you anticipated.

So now you're staring at your actual take-home pay. It doesn't reflect the long nights grading or weekends spent prepping lessons. It barely covers rent, groceries, gas, and a student loan payment. Maybe you're supporting a family. Maybe you're the first in your household to ever land a professional job and others are relying on you. Maybe you just want to save for a down payment on a home one day. Regardless, it becomes clear: teaching is not just emotionally taxing—it requires a financial plan that few are trained to create. This is where many teachers hit a wall. They either go into survival mode or shut down completely, hoping things will somehow work out. But "hoping" is not a strategy. Clarity is.

Understanding where your money goes is the first step in reclaiming control. This chapter will break down each component of a teacher's paycheck with plain-language explanations. We'll decode your deductions and walk through the structure of your benefits. We'll talk about why some teachers are eligible for Social Security and others are not, how your state retirement system works (and what it doesn't cover), and how to spot financial leaks in your benefits package. You'll learn how to calculate your net pay, how to project it forward over the year, and how to begin organizing your budget around your actual income—not the fantasy number at the top of your contract.

But this chapter isn't just about numbers. It's about real life. That paycheck represents more than compensation. It represents your value, your time, your choices, and the limitations you didn't create but must now navigate. Whether you're a single teacher, part of a dual-educator household, or raising kids while supporting aging parents, this chapter is about giving you the awareness and confidence to make the most of your money from day one. It will prepare you to take the next financial step, not with fear or frustration, but with clarity and ownership of your financial story.

Let's talk about how your payment schedule can affect your cash flow. Are you paid once a month? Bi-weekly? On the 15th and 30th? Many teachers aren't prepared for the inconsistency of payment cycles, especially when summer months don't include paychecks unless you've elected to stretch your pay over 12 months instead of 10. That choice alone can significantly impact your ability to plan for expenses, save, or avoid credit card debt during those income gaps.

You should also examine whether you're truly maximizing your benefits. Are you contributing to your 403(b) or 457 plan? Do you know what kind of match your district offers, if any? These are retirement accounts that often go underutilized by teachers who are so focused on the here-and-now that they miss opportunities to build their future. In this chapter, we'll look at how to begin investing, even if it's just $25 per paycheck, and how that habit can grow into long-term security.

There's also the psychological side of that first paycheck. It doesn't feel like you expected it to. You're doing something meaningful, something hard, something that requires immense skill—and you're being compensated like it doesn't matter. That disconnect can lead to burnout, bitterness, and detachment. It can tempt you to overspend on the weekend just to feel a sense of relief. We'll name those emotions here. We'll validate them. But we'll also move beyond them, into a framework of response rather than reaction.

Throughout this chapter, we'll also explore what happens when your paycheck is called on to do more than pay bills. Maybe you're paying for your own classroom supplies. Maybe you're contributing to family members' needs, or trying to make sure your own children can access opportunities you never had. This isn't just about money management. It's about mission management. And unless you have a plan, it's easy to give everything away and leave yourself with nothing.

By the end of this chapter, my hope is that you see your paycheck not just as a frustrating piece of paper or digital statement, but as a document of power—one that you can learn from, plan around, and ultimately reshape to serve *you*. Because when you understand where your money is going, you can begin to decide where it goes next.

Chapter 2: Understanding Your Pay Stub, Contract, and Benefits as a New Teacher

Getting your first teaching job feels like a major milestone—and it is. You sign a contract, get your classroom keys, start prepping for students, and receive that long-anticipated email from HR with your salary, benefits, and deductions. But very quickly, excitement can turn into confusion. You glance at your pay stub or benefits sheet and realize you don't fully understand what you signed up for. Numbers don't seem to line up. Deductions come out of nowhere. The contract you thought was clear now reads like a different language. This chapter exists to translate it all. To help you make sense of what your employment agreement actually means for your money.

Let's start with the salary number—because it's rarely as straightforward as it seems. Your contract might say $45,000 or $52,000 or $61,000 per year, but how that gets paid to you depends on your district's payroll schedule. Are you being paid on a 10-month calendar or a 12-month cycle? Are you receiving bi-weekly paychecks or just once a month? The number on your contract is your gross annual salary—not your take-home pay. Understanding the difference between what you're offered and what actually arrives in your bank account is the foundation of everything else.

Next comes your pay stub—and it deserves more than a glance. It's a map of your compensation. Each line tells a story: federal withholding, state tax, retirement contributions, health insurance premiums, union dues, and maybe other deductions like optional disability insurance or cafeteria plan benefits. Each district formats pay stubs a little differently, but the structure is the same: gross income, deductions, and net pay. If you don't understand what each deduction is for, you're not alone—but learning how to read this document is one of the most empowering things you can do as a professional.

Your retirement plan is one of the most significant deductions on that stub. Many teachers contribute to a state retirement system, which functions as a pension plan. In states with Teacher Retirement Systems (TRS or STRS), a fixed percentage of your paycheck—often 6-8%—is automatically deducted. In return, you'll receive a monthly pension after meeting specific service and age requirements. This is a powerful benefit, but it comes with trade-offs: limited flexibility, long vesting periods, and reduced access to Social Security in some states. Understanding how this plan works is key to making smart choices about additional savings vehicles like 403(b) and 457 plans.

Speaking of benefits, let's talk health insurance. Your district likely offers multiple plan tiers with varying premiums, deductibles, and out-of-pocket costs. Don't just pick the cheapest plan—consider your personal healthcare needs, your family situation, and what kind of coverage offers the best protection. Also explore whether your district offers supplemental insurance (dental, vision, life, disability), and learn which of these are worth enrolling in during your benefits window. Some plans are essential safeguards; others may not be necessary depending on your circumstances.

Then there's your contract itself. It outlines your working conditions, salary schedule, evaluation process, leave policies, and obligations. Pay special attention to language around tenure, step increases, sick leave accumulation, and how retirement benefits are affected by years of service. If you're in a union district, understand what the collective bargaining agreement provides. If you're not unionized, you'll need to understand what protections and support systems are (or aren't) in place should you need help or encounter disputes.

One of the most overlooked aspects of your contract is how future earnings are structured. Are there automatic raises based on years of experience or continuing education credits? What is the pay scale for a master's degree or national board certification? Knowing this helps you plan for income growth over time. And if your district offers stipends for coaching, advising clubs, or teaching summer school, those can be strategic ways to increase your income if needed.

You should also understand the timing of your benefits. When do your retirement contributions begin? When do your health benefits start? Are you covered immediately or after a probationary period? When do raises and step increases kick in? These timing details matter when you're making financial plans for the next 6-12 months, especially if you're transitioning from student life or another career.

It's also important to know what your district offers beyond pay and insurance. Do you have access to financial wellness programs? Is there a credit union you can join? Are there options for flexible spending accounts (FSAs) or health savings accounts (HSAs)? What tuition reimbursement or professional development funding is available? These seemingly small benefits can have a big impact on your bottom line.

This chapter isn't about turning you into an HR specialist—it's about making sure you're not caught off guard. Because your paycheck, your contract, and your benefits are not just administrative paperwork. They are the foundation of your financial life. When you understand them fully, you're no longer guessing. You're planning. You're adjusting. You're advocating for yourself. And most importantly, you're making every part of your compensation work for *you*.

Chapter 3: 403(b), 457, and Pensions – A Beginner's Guide to School Retirement Plans

If there is one financial topic that makes new teachers glaze over faster than taxes, it's retirement plans. The acronyms alone are intimidating: 403(b), 457(b), TRS, STRS, ERS, IRA. But here's the truth: understanding your retirement options early on can completely change your financial future. Because the earlier you understand what each of these plans does, how they work, and which ones you control, the better positioned you'll be to build the kind of retirement that reflects the life you want to live when you're done teaching full-time.

Let's begin with the pension plan—the benefit many teachers are automatically enrolled in and often misunderstand. A pension is a defined benefit plan, meaning you are promised a monthly income in retirement based on a formula. That formula typically considers your years of service, your final average salary, and a multiplier determined by your state's retirement system. Unlike a 401(k), which depends on market performance and individual investment choices, a pension gives you a predictable income stream for life. But there's a catch: you usually have to stay in the system for 5 to 10 years to become vested, and if you leave before then, you may forfeit those benefits.

Then there's the 403(b), a defined contribution plan often referred to as the "teacher's 401(k)." This is a retirement plan that you control. You choose how much to contribute and, in many cases, how to invest that money. The money you put into a traditional 403(b) comes out of your paycheck before taxes, reducing your taxable income now but requiring taxes later in retirement. Some districts also offer a Roth 403(b) option, where you pay taxes on the money now but withdraw it tax-free later. Many teachers don't know this plan exists, or they ignore it because they think their pension is enough. But here's the reality: for most modern educators, the pension alone won't cover everything. You will need supplemental savings to retire with dignity and flexibility.

The 457(b) is another voluntary retirement plan, and it's often underutilized. What makes it powerful is that you can contribute to a 403(b) and a 457(b) at the same time—essentially doubling your tax-advantaged retirement savings. The 457(b) has one major benefit many teachers overlook: there is no early withdrawal penalty if you leave your job and access funds before age 59½. That makes it a valuable tool for teachers who plan to retire early, switch careers, or step away from the classroom for personal reasons.

Now let's compare these options. Your pension is automatic, but it requires a long-term commitment. The 403(b) gives you control, but it demands initiative and a willingness to understand investment basics. The 457(b) offers unique flexibility, but not every district offers it. Each plan has pros and cons. The pension rewards stability and loyalty. The 403(b) empowers growth. The 457(b) offers agility. The real power is in understanding how these options work *together*, not in isolation.

Unfortunately, many teachers don't take full advantage of these plans because no one sits down and explains them in plain language. HR departments are often too stretched to provide one-on-one financial education. Vendors may focus more on sales than on service. That's why you need to be your own advocate. Start by asking questions: What is the vesting schedule for my pension? Does my district offer a 403(b) match? Who administers my plan? What are the fees? What investment options are available to me? This isn't about becoming an expert—it's about being informed enough to make decisions that benefit you, not just your employer.

It's also worth considering what happens if your life changes. What if you move to another state? What if you take time off to raise children or care for a loved one? What if you retire early or switch careers altogether? Pensions aren't portable across state lines, and many teachers lose years of retirement credit by transferring districts or leaving the profession. This is why having your own retirement account, like a 403(b) or 457(b), becomes not just helpful—but essential. You need something that follows *you*, no matter where you go.

Let's also be clear: retirement planning isn't just for people in their 50s. It's for every teacher who wants to eventually stop working and still have a roof over their head, groceries in the fridge, and a life they enjoy. Even if you can only contribute $25 per paycheck, do it. Build the habit. Watch the balance grow. This is how you create future options, and future peace.

Finally, understand that this chapter isn't about selling a one-size-fits-all solution. Some teachers stay 30 years and rely on their pension. Others move states, change careers, or retire early and need a different structure. What matters is that you know what tools are available to you—and that you use them on your terms, with eyes wide open. Because when you understand your retirement options, you don't just plan for the end of your career. You begin designing the life you want to live after the classroom.

Chapter 4: Pension Plans 101 – How They Work, When They Work, and What to Watch For

Pensions are one of the few remaining retirement benefits in America that promise a guaranteed income for life—and for many teachers, that promise is what keeps them in the classroom through the toughest years. But while the concept of a pension sounds comforting, the details are often confusing, overlooked, or misunderstood. If you've ever wondered whether your pension will actually be enough to live on, or how it works if you change districts or leave teaching altogether, this chapter will give you the clarity and confidence to understand what your pension really means.

Let's start with the basics. A pension is a defined benefit retirement plan. That means your future benefit is calculated using a formula, not dependent on how well the stock market performs or how much you contribute individually. Most teacher pensions are based on a formula like: Final Average Salary x Years of Service x Multiplier. For example, if you work 30 years, earn a final average salary of $60,000, and your multiplier is 2.0%, your annual pension would be $36,000. That benefit is paid out every year for the rest of your life after retirement.

But it's not automatic. You must meet specific eligibility requirements, including a minimum number of years in the system—called vesting—and a certain age before you can access your full benefit. In many states, you must work at least 5 to 10 years just to be vested. Leave before that and you may walk away with nothing more than your own contributions. And even after vesting, early retirement usually results in a reduced benefit. This makes your pension a long-game investment, not a short-term reward.

Another important factor is that most teacher pensions do not include Social Security. In about 15 states, public school teachers don't contribute to Social Security and therefore may not receive Social Security benefits unless they have enough non-teaching work history. Even if you do qualify, your teacher pension can trigger something called the Windfall Elimination Provision (WEP), which reduces your Social Security benefit. This is a critical point to understand, especially if you were counting on having both a pension and full Social Security income in retirement.

Now let's talk about what can go wrong. One of the biggest misconceptions teachers have is that their pension is automatically "enough." But depending on your lifestyle, healthcare costs, and inflation, your pension might only cover the basics. There are no guarantees that it will keep pace with cost-of-living increases. Some plans offer cost-of-living adjustments (COLAs), but many do not—and the ones that do may freeze or change over time. Without a supplemental savings strategy, many retired teachers find themselves in a financial squeeze.

Another pitfall is portability. Your pension benefit usually only grows if you stay in the same retirement system. If you move across state lines or take a job in another district with a different system, your years of service may not transfer. That means starting over with the vesting clock, and potentially losing thousands in long-term retirement value. If you anticipate moving during your career, it may be wise to rely less on your pension and more on portable savings options like a 403(b) or Roth IRA.

To navigate these systems well, you must become an active participant in your retirement planning. Don't assume someone else is managing it for you. Request your pension estimate annually. Learn your vesting date. Understand your system's benefit calculator and play out different retirement scenarios. Talk to HR. Join a pension seminar if your district or union offers one. This is your future income—you deserve to know what it will (and won't) do for you.

It also matters how and when you retire. Some pension plans allow you to choose between different payout options: single life, joint survivor, or period certain. Each has trade-offs. A single life annuity gives you the largest monthly payment but stops when you die. A joint survivor annuity continues to pay your spouse but offers a lower monthly benefit. Period certain options guarantee payment for a set number of years. These decisions should be made in context with your overall retirement plan, your spouse's income, and your other assets.

Finally, ask yourself what role you want your pension to play in your broader financial picture. It can be your financial foundation, but it should not be the only floor you stand on. Supplementing it with a 403(b), 457, or IRA gives you more control, more flexibility, and more protection against inflation or policy changes. The pension is a promise—but your savings are your power. Use both.

By the end of this chapter, my goal isn't just for you to understand your pension—it's for you to feel confident engaging with it. To make it part of your plan, not just a question mark on your pay stub. To see it not just as a benefit you've earned, but a piece of the freedom you're building. Because teaching is hard work. Retirement shouldn't be a mystery.

Chapter 5: Defined Contribution vs. Defined Benefit – When to Pick One Over the Other

One of the most important financial decisions a teacher can make involves understanding the difference between a defined benefit plan and a defined contribution plan. If you're already enrolled in a pension system, you might assume the choice is made for you—but in many districts and states, especially for new hires or those changing jobs, there are options. And the option you choose can shape your retirement income, your financial flexibility, and your peace of mind. This chapter exists to walk you through that decision without pressure or confusion.

A defined benefit plan is what most people think of as a traditional pension. It promises a guaranteed monthly income in retirement, calculated using a formula that includes your years of service, your final average salary, and a multiplier specific to your state or district. The plan is managed by a government entity, and you have little control over the investments. The trade-off? In exchange for less control, you get predictable income for life—as long as you stay long enough to be vested and retire under the system's rules.

A defined contribution plan, by contrast, is more like a 403(b), 401(k), or 457 plan. You decide how much to contribute, and you often have a menu of investment options to choose from. Your future retirement income depends on how much you contribute, how those investments perform, and how long your money has to grow. There are no guarantees, but there is flexibility. If you change careers, switch states, or leave the classroom, you can take your money with you.

Here's where it gets tricky: some school districts offer new hires a choice between these two types of plans. That might sound like a great opportunity, but it's also a weighty decision. If you expect to stay in the same school system or state for 25 to 30 years, a defined benefit plan can offer tremendous value. But if you plan to relocate, change careers, or if you're entering teaching later in life, a defined contribution plan might offer more control and portability. It all depends on your goals, your career timeline, and your tolerance for risk.

Let's break down the pros and cons. A defined benefit plan offers stability, but requires long-term commitment and trust in the system. It typically does not allow early access to funds, and you might lose significant value if you leave before retirement age. Defined contribution plans, on the other hand, allow for earlier access, more personal control, and the ability to customize your investment strategy—but they come with market risk and no guaranteed lifetime income.

There's also the question of survivor benefits. Some pension plans offer continued payments to a spouse after your death, but that often comes at the cost of a reduced monthly benefit. Defined contribution plans, however, allow your remaining balance to be inherited by beneficiaries, offering more flexibility for family financial planning. If you're single, married, or have children, this may play a role in your decision.

Another consideration is inflation protection. Many pension systems do not offer automatic cost-of-living adjustments (COLAs), or offer them only occasionally. That means your fixed monthly income might lose purchasing power over time. With a defined contribution plan, you can structure withdrawals and investments to attempt to keep pace with inflation, though this again requires active planning.

Teachers also need to consider how these plans affect Social Security. In states where teachers don't participate in Social Security, the defined benefit plan becomes even more important—but also more precarious if you don't stay long enough to vest. If you do participate in Social Security, your defined contribution savings can serve as a powerful third leg to your retirement income stool, alongside Social Security and your pension or 403(b).

So when should you pick one over the other? Choose a defined benefit plan if you are confident you will spend the majority of your career in one system, if you prefer guaranteed income over flexibility, and if you value predictability over personal control. Choose a defined contribution plan if you anticipate mobility, want more direct control over your retirement savings, or want to tailor your investments to your personal risk tolerance.

Ultimately, there is no universally right answer. What matters is that you understand what each option offers, what it limits, and how it aligns with your goals. If you're unsure, talk to a trusted financial advisor who understands public school retirement systems. Your retirement shouldn't be left to guesswork. Whether you choose the reliability of a defined benefit or the control of a defined contribution, this decision should be made on purpose—with your future in mind, not just your present.

Chapter 6: Budgeting on a Modest Salary – Every Dollar Needs a Job

Let's start with a truth many teachers carry quietly: budgeting on a teacher's salary isn't about laziness, irresponsibility, or living beyond your means. It's about reality. The reality is that the salary structure of most school districts asks educators to do professional-level work—with advanced degrees and lifelong impact—on wages that often don't reflect that value. And yet, within this limitation, teachers still show up, still serve, and still stretch every dollar to support their students and their families. This chapter is about reclaiming that stretch. It's about turning survival into strategy.

The first mindset shift is this: your budget is not a punishment. It's a plan. It's not there to scold you or shame you. It's a tool that helps you tell your money where to go instead of wondering where it went. Budgeting doesn't mean giving up joy. It means giving every dollar a job—so that joy can be part of the plan, not an afterthought squeezed into whatever's left over. A good teacher budget doesn't just track expenses. It reflects values, supports goals, and builds confidence over time.

Start with the basics: income and expenses. Know exactly what you bring home every month—not what your contract says, but what actually lands in your account after taxes, insurance, and retirement contributions. Then lay out your fixed costs: rent or mortgage, utilities, transportation, minimum loan payments. Next, add in variable categories: groceries, gas, classroom supplies (yes, that deserves its own line), and spending money. Too many teachers forget to budget for the money they spend on their students. A budget that ignores that reality is doomed to fail.

Once you've captured the essentials, identify your financial priorities. Is it getting out of credit card debt? Saving for a home? Building a three-month emergency fund? Contributing to a Roth IRA? Your priorities shape your plan. If everything is a priority, nothing is. Choose one to two main focuses per quarter or semester and build your budget to reflect that. You can shift later, but clarity up front helps you move forward instead of spinning in circles.

Now let's talk about the guilt factor. Teachers often feel guilty spending money on themselves. They defer self-care, professional development, and even basic needs because they feel like every extra dollar should go to the classroom. But here's the truth: you cannot pour from an empty cup. Your well-being matters. Your future matters. And your budget should make room for that. Even if it's just $20 a month into a vacation fund or a massage every few months, budgeting for joy helps prevent burnout—and that matters as much as any worksheet you print for your students.

On a modest salary, budgeting also requires adaptability. Summer breaks, changes in contract hours, or inconsistent stipends can throw off even the best-laid plans. Consider using a "zero-based budget" model, where every dollar is assigned a job ahead of time, and monthly changes are accounted for. Use envelopes (physical or digital), category caps, or percentage rules to stay consistent. Tools like YNAB (You Need a Budget), EveryDollar, or a basic spreadsheet can help structure your system. The method matters less than the commitment to checking in regularly.

Another helpful strategy is thinking in terms of cash flow and timing. If you're paid once a month, your budget should stretch differently than if you're paid bi-weekly. Map out which bills are due when, and avoid overdrafts or shortfalls by knowing exactly what part of your paycheck covers which part of your month. Many teachers find it helpful to create a visual calendar or use bill-pay features to automate what they can. Reduce friction. Increase predictability.

Let's not forget the power of community. Consider budgeting as a household if you share expenses, and have regular financial check-ins with your partner or spouse. For two-teacher households, budgeting as a team is crucial. Agree on your values, then allocate your income accordingly. Even if you're single, find someone who can serve as an accountability partner. Financial literacy doesn't have to be lonely.

And when the money just doesn't stretch far enough, approach the situation with compassion—not blame. Sometimes budgeting reveals a gap that no spreadsheet can fix. In those cases, the next step may be seeking supplemental income, negotiating a higher-paying position within the district, or exploring public service loan forgiveness to reduce burdens. Budgeting is not just about restriction—it's a signal system. If the signals tell you something has to change, listen with clarity, not shame.

The real win isn't just having a perfectly balanced spreadsheet. It's the peace that comes from knowing where your money goes. It's the power of making decisions on purpose. And it's the freedom of knowing you're not working this hard without a plan. Budgeting on a teacher's salary may require creativity, sacrifice, and adaptability. But with the right mindset and tools, it can also become a source of control, calm, and quiet confidence—one paycheck at a time.

Chapter 7: What No One Tells You About Credit – Building It, Using It, and Protecting It

Credit is one of those things we're expected to understand, yet few people ever receive a clear, compassionate, or complete explanation of how it actually works. For teachers, especially those who entered the field with student debt or inconsistent early income, credit can feel more like a shadow than a tool. You might carry guilt about past missed payments or confusion about why your score dropped after you paid off a loan. This chapter won't shame you or talk down to you. It's here to illuminate the systems, demystify the score, and show you how to use credit in a way that supports your financial life—not controls it.

Let's start with the basics: your credit score is essentially a trust score. It tells lenders how reliably you've borrowed and repaid money. But the formula behind that number isn't always intuitive. Paying off a loan early might seem like a good thing—and for your bank account, it is. But it could cause a small dip in your score because one of the factors in credit scoring is the length and variety of active accounts. That's not a reason to avoid paying off debt. It's a reason to stop taking your score personally. Your goal isn't to game the system; it's to understand it well enough that it doesn't stand in your way.

There are five major components to a credit score: payment history (35%), amounts owed (30%), length of credit history (15%), new credit (10%), and credit mix (10%). Teachers often have stable payment habits but may struggle with the mix and utilization pieces. If you're only using one credit card, for example, or if your total debt load is close to your limits—even if you pay on time—your score can suffer. Understanding these components helps you see credit as a system to be managed rather than a mystery to fear.

Credit reports and credit scores are not the same thing. Your credit report is a detailed record of your borrowing history, while your score is a number generated from that data. Teachers should review their credit reports annually from the three major bureaus: Equifax, Experian, and TransUnion. Mistakes are surprisingly common, and fixing them can improve your score. A missed payment that was incorrectly reported or a closed account that still shows a balance are not just errors—they're obstacles to your financial momentum.

Building credit from scratch—or rebuilding it after hardship—requires strategy, not luck. One way to start is with a secured credit card. You deposit a small amount of money, which becomes your credit limit. Use the card for something small each month, like gas or groceries, and pay it off in full. Over time, this builds a positive history. Another method is becoming an authorized user on a family member's well-managed credit card. Their good credit behavior can help boost your score, without you needing to carry the debt or responsibility yourself.

Using credit wisely means borrowing with intention. Just because you can qualify for a store card doesn't mean you should open one. Many teachers are tempted by classroom supply discounts or promotional offers, but multiple hard inquiries in a short span can lower your score. Instead, be selective. Choose one or two general-purpose cards with strong reputations and low fees. Set up automatic payments for at least the minimum due to avoid late fees. Then pay more than the minimum whenever possible to reduce interest costs and build good habits.

Credit protection is just as important as credit building. Teachers are not immune to identity theft. In fact, your personal information is often on multiple school systems, HR platforms, and professional websites. Freeze your credit at all three bureaus when you're not actively applying for new credit. It's free and reversible. Set up fraud alerts and monitor your accounts regularly. These steps may seem tedious, but they are an act of financial self-defense in a world where breaches happen every day.

One of the most misunderstood areas of credit is how it affects your insurance, housing, and even employment. Some school districts, especially charter or private institutions, may review credit as part of the hiring process. Insurance companies often use credit-based insurance scores to set premiums. Landlords look at credit reports when evaluating rental applications. This doesn't mean a low score will ruin your life—but it does mean that credit has power far beyond just loans and cards. Knowing this gives you an edge.

Let's also name the emotional side of credit. For many teachers, especially those who entered the profession through alternative certification or after a career change, credit can carry shame. Maybe you had to use credit cards to float unpaid internships or summer gaps. Maybe you missed a few payments during student teaching. You are not your score. Credit is a number, not a measure of your worth. What matters now is how you move forward. Progress begins with knowledge, and knowledge removes fear.

Here's where to start this month: pull your credit reports for free from annualcreditreport.com. Dispute any errors you find. Set calendar reminders to pay every bill on time. If your credit usage is over 30%, work on paying down balances. If you don't have a credit card yet, consider starting with a secured one. And above all, reframe your thinking: credit is a tool. Used wisely, it can help you buy a home, qualify for better rates, and increase your financial security. Let it work for you—not against you.

Chapter 8: Renting or Buying? How to Think About Housing as a New Teacher

Let's start by acknowledging something most people won't say out loud: housing decisions for teachers aren't just about money. They're about time, energy, safety, stress, and often a deep emotional tie to the communities where we work. It's easy for financial "gurus" to say, "Buy as soon as you can," but they're not grading papers until 10 PM, waking up at 5 AM, or navigating public school salaries. Whether you're renting a studio near your school or trying to save for a down payment, your choices are not just about wealth-building—they're about survival and stability, too. This chapter is here to guide you through the real-life, teacher-specific factors that should shape your housing decisions.

Renting may not build equity, but for many teachers, it provides flexibility, lower upfront costs, and the ability to live closer to work. If your district pays $47,000 and the average home near your school costs $450,000, buying might not just be a stretch—it might be financially destabilizing. Teachers often don't have tens of thousands of dollars for a down payment, closing costs, and moving expenses. And renting doesn't mean you're financially illiterate or falling behind—it may mean you're choosing peace, predictability, and a short commute over debt, risk, and a fixer-upper with hidden costs.

Buying, on the other hand, can be a powerful tool for long-term wealth building—if the numbers make sense. Over time, mortgage payments can stay fixed while rents rise, and owning property gives you the opportunity to build equity, deduct mortgage interest, and create a stable home base. But new teachers should tread carefully. If you're on a probationary contract, if your job isn't guaranteed past the school year, or if you're considering relocating for better pay or district culture, buying too soon can trap you financially and geographically. Your first few years in the classroom are about finding your rhythm—not locking yourself into a 30-year commitment.

There's also the emotional math. Many teachers feel pressure to buy a home because it feels like a rite of adulthood. But ownership comes with hidden costs: property taxes, repairs, HOA fees, insurance, and maintenance. One broken furnace or cracked foundation can wipe out your emergency fund overnight. If you're still paying off student loans, building a retirement fund, or supporting family, these extra housing expenses can tip your financial balance. Renting doesn't mean you're standing still—it may mean you're protecting your future by not overreaching in the present.

Another layer to this decision is your support system. Do you have a family member who can help with the down payment? Are you moving in with a partner who already owns property? Are you co-signing with a parent? These relational dynamics change the equation—but they also introduce risk. Buying with someone else (whether a spouse, partner, or family member) means shared ownership, shared debt, and shared financial exposure. It's crucial to be clear on titles, responsibilities, exit strategies, and long-term intentions before you enter into a mortgage with someone else.

Let's talk credit and mortgage qualification. Many new teachers are surprised to learn that even with a full-time teaching job, they don't qualify for the mortgage they expected. Lenders want to see stable income, decent credit, and a manageable debt-to-income ratio. If you're carrying student loans, auto payments, or credit card debt, your borrowing power may be limited—even if your rent would be the same as a mortgage. If buying is your goal, one of the best things you can do in your early teaching years is build your credit, reduce unnecessary debt, and understand what mortgage products you might qualify for down the road.

Geography also plays a big role. In some states, teacher housing stipends or programs may support homeownership. In others, housing costs are so out of sync with teacher pay that renting is the only feasible option. If you teach in a city with high cost of living but want to buy, you may have to look 30+ miles away—and trade your time and energy for affordability. That commute has a cost. It's not just gas or tolls—it's grading in your car, showing up tired to parent-teacher night, or missing your own kid's soccer game. Don't let the promise of equity-building cost you your quality of life.

So how do you decide? Start by taking a brutally honest look at your budget. Do you know your monthly take-home pay after taxes and retirement contributions? Do you have an emergency fund? Do you have any savings beyond your classroom setup expenses? Run the numbers, and don't forget to factor in hidden costs like home maintenance, insurance premiums, and property taxes. Then look at your timeline. Are you planning to stay in your district for five years or more? Or are you still figuring out your career path and location? Buying only makes sense if the math works *and* your life stage supports it.

Action steps? Start small. Pull your credit report. Talk to HR about housing programs or partnerships with local banks. Set a monthly savings goal for your down payment—even if it's $100. Track what you're spending on rent and compare it to estimated mortgage payments *with* taxes and insurance. Interview teachers in your area who have bought homes—ask what they wish they knew. And if you're renting, be smart about your lease: understand your renewal terms, avoid predatory increases, and take good care of your space to keep your housing costs stable.

The goal is not to rent or to buy. The goal is to feel safe, stable, and financially grounded in your housing choice. There is no shame in taking your time. There is wisdom in waiting. And there is power in knowing that whichever path you choose, you can make it work with knowledge, planning, and clarity. This isn't about what others say you should do. It's about what works for your life, your budget, and your long-term goals as a teacher building not just a classroom, but a life.

Chapter 9: Teacher Insurance Basics – Auto, Home, Health, and Disability

If there's one topic that reliably puts people to sleep, it's insurance. But if you're a teacher trying to build a life on a modest salary, insurance isn't a boring detail—it's a financial backbone. Without the right insurance, one car accident, one house fire, one surgery, or one injury could wipe out years of careful budgeting. This chapter is not about fear-mongering. It's about protection. It's about thinking like the responsible educator you are, planning for life's unexpected moments so you can move forward with less anxiety and more freedom. You already carry the weight of your classroom. You don't need to carry unnecessary financial risk too.

Let's start with auto insurance because for most teachers, the car is non-negotiable. It's how you get to school, get to meetings, get your kids to daycare, and occasionally escape to Target or a Friday night football game. You need coverage that actually covers you—not just the cheapest premium you could find in a panic when you bought your last car. Understand the difference between liability, comprehensive, and collision coverage. Know your deductible. And if you're relying on your car daily, skip the state minimums and pay a little more for peace of mind. A hit-and-run in the school parking lot or a deer on your rural drive home is not the time to discover you're underinsured.

Next up is homeowners or renters insurance. If you own your home, you already know that a busted water heater or hailstorm can wreck your finances if you're not protected. But even if you rent, don't skip coverage.

Your landlord's insurance does not cover your things. That classroom library you've been building with your own money? Your laptop, your furniture, your clothes? If a fire breaks out or someone breaks in, renters insurance can mean the difference between devastation and a manageable setback. And it usually costs less than a dinner out.

Health insurance deserves more than a cursory glance during your HR orientation. It's often the most expensive and most important benefit you have. Start by understanding the basics: premium, deductible, co-pay, co-insurance, and out-of-pocket maximum. Then go deeper. Do you understand the difference between an HMO and a PPO? Is your favorite doctor in-network? Are you paying for more coverage than you need, or too little? Many teachers stick with the default plan without considering their actual medical needs. Don't be afraid to ask HR questions. This is your money and your body. Treat both with respect.

Disability insurance is the sleeper hit of this chapter. Most people ignore it until they're in crisis. But for teachers—who use their voices, backs, and brains every day—it matters deeply. A back injury, chronic illness, or mental health episode can take you out of the classroom for weeks or months. Without disability coverage, your paycheck could dry up just when you need it most. Short-term and long-term disability plans vary widely, and what your district offers may not be enough. Consider a private policy if needed, especially if you're the main breadwinner. This is about income protection, not just health.

Every type of insurance carries trade-offs. Higher premiums usually mean lower deductibles and better coverage—but they eat into your monthly cash flow. Skimping on coverage saves money now, but could cost you far more later. The goal is to find a balance that works for your actual life, not some theoretical budget. Think about your commute, your home, your health history, your support system. Financial literacy isn't about perfection—it's about personalization.

If you're in a two-teacher household, coordinate your plans. You might not need double coverage in every area. One spouse might carry the health plan while the other picks up the better disability insurance. Talk openly about what each of you has, what gaps exist, and where you're duplicating. This is not just about saving money; it's about making sure neither of you is exposed unnecessarily. Team up, like you do with lesson planning or parent-teacher night.

There's also the issue of beneficiaries. Who gets the payout if something happens to you? Many people list a parent or sibling when they're young and forget to update it. If you're married, divorced, have children, or care for someone financially, make sure your insurance policies reflect your reality. An outdated beneficiary can cause legal nightmares for your loved ones. Set a calendar reminder to review these annually. It's five minutes that can save your family five months of stress.

Another blind spot? Policy bundling. Some insurance companies offer discounts when you bundle auto, home, and even life insurance. But those discounts aren't always what they seem. Sometimes a bundled plan is still more expensive than shopping each policy separately. Use an independent agent or online comparison tool to run the numbers. Don't confuse convenience with cost-efficiency. What worked for you three years ago may not be working now.

Finally, take notes. Make an insurance folder—digital or physical. Include copies of your policies, contact info for your agents, a running list of your deductibles, and any claims you've filed. You'll thank yourself the next time you're dealing with a cracked windshield or scheduling a surgery. More importantly, you'll feel less like a passenger in your financial life and more like the one driving. Insurance doesn't have to be intimidating. For teachers, it can be one of the most empowering tools in your toolbox.

Chapter 10: Life Insurance for Teachers – Why You Might Need It Sooner Than You Think

You became a teacher to make a difference, not to think about your mortality. But life has a way of making the unexpected feel urgent, and that's why we need to talk about life insurance. Not because you're planning for something grim, but because protecting the people you love—your partner, your kids, your parents, your students—starts with planning ahead. Life insurance is one of those things you don't think you need until it's too late. And yet, for educators, it might be one of the most powerful financial tools in your toolkit, especially if you're trying to create some peace of mind on a modest income.

Let's start with a reality check: many school districts offer some level of group life insurance, often a flat amount like $10,000 or one to two times your salary. That might sound decent on paper, but if you have dependents—children, a spouse, or even parents who rely on your income—it won't come close to covering their financial needs if something happens to you. Think about mortgage or rent payments, childcare, student loans, funeral expenses, and day-to-day bills. The true cost of losing your income stretches far beyond one year's salary. That's why supplemental life insurance is something you should seriously consider, especially in your 20s, 30s, and 40s when rates are low and your health is (hopefully) good.

There are two main types of life insurance: term and whole life. Term life insurance is straightforward—you pay for coverage over a fixed period (say,

20 or 30 years), and if you pass away during that time, your beneficiaries receive the payout. It's affordable, flexible, and excellent for young teachers who want to protect their families during their earning years. Whole life insurance, on the other hand, is more expensive and includes a savings component, sometimes sold as an investment. It sounds appealing, but for most teachers, term life offers more bang for your buck—and the extra money can be put toward retirement, debt payoff, or an emergency fund.

Don't fall into the trap of thinking that life insurance is only necessary if you have kids. If you have a partner who depends on your income, cosigned student loans, or even a sibling who would handle your affairs, your absence could create both emotional and financial turmoil. A life insurance policy can help cover final expenses, prevent your loved ones from going into debt, and give them space to grieve without immediately worrying about money. And here's something no one tells you: if you wait until a health diagnosis, it may be too late to qualify. That's why buying early matters.

Another question that comes up a lot: should you just take the insurance your district provides, or get your own policy? District plans are usually convenient but limited. They may not be portable if you switch schools or retire early. A personal policy, by contrast, travels with you. It gives you continuity and flexibility. And with term policies being so affordable (sometimes less than $20/month for healthy young teachers), it's an investment in stability that won't break the bank.

If you're part of a two-teacher household, you might assume that you don't need as much coverage because you both bring in income. But what if one of you passes away and the other has to take unpaid time off, manage the kids solo, or relocate to be near family? Life insurance isn't just about income replacement. It's about creating breathing room—space to adjust without financial panic. That's the kind of support that money actually can buy.

Some teachers worry that buying life insurance is morbid or superstitious, as if planning for death somehow invites it. But it's really the opposite. Getting a life insurance policy is one of the most optimistic things you can do. It says: I believe in my future. I believe that the people I care about deserve to be protected. I believe I have something worth insuring. That's not fear—that's love with a plan.

Here's a simple action plan: first, calculate your basic needs. A good rule of thumb is 10-12 times your annual income, but adjust that for debt, dependents, and whether your spouse also works. Then, shop around. Look for policies from reputable providers and use online calculators to compare rates. If your budget is tight, start with a smaller policy and increase coverage as your salary grows. Even $100,000 in coverage is better than none. And once you have a policy, review it every few years as your life changes.

Lastly, be sure your beneficiaries are up-to-date, and that someone knows where to find your policy documents. Life insurance only works if your people can access it. Don't let your efforts go to waste because of missed paperwork or outdated contact information. And remember: this isn't a one-and-done decision. It's a living part of your financial plan, just like your retirement savings and your emergency fund.

Part II – The Middle Years: Growing Income, Growing Responsibility

Part II of *Financial Literacy For Teachers* enters the critical phase of a teacher's financial life—the middle years. These are the years where income begins to rise, but so does the weight of responsibility. Teachers in this stage may be navigating dual incomes, raising children, managing student loans, saving for a home (or paying one off), planning for retirement, and sometimes supporting aging parents—all while staying committed to their classrooms. Financial decisions start to carry more long-term impact, and missteps can feel harder to recover from.

This section is designed to guide educators through the nuances of this complex chapter in life. We dive into real-world topics like how to balance pension contributions with day-to-day living expenses, whether to rent or buy based on long-term district plans, and how to make sense of different types of retirement accounts (403(b), Roth IRA, etc.). You'll learn how to evaluate benefit packages, navigate marriage and taxes as educators, make smart insurance choices, and approach credit building with clarity—not confusion.

What makes this section different is its recognition of the emotional and logistical reality of teaching through your 30s, 40s, and early 50s. We aren't just giving financial advice—we're offering a roadmap for how to build wealth while managing competing priorities and systemic pressures. Whether you're planning for kids, preparing for leadership roles, or considering a side hustle, these chapters meet you where you are with grounded, judgment-free guidance.

You don't need to do it all perfectly. But you do need to understand the systems you're in—and how to make those systems work for *you*. This part of the book helps you do just that.

Chapter 11: From Novice to Experienced – Your Income Grows, So Should Your Strategy

The early years of teaching are about survival. You're learning the curriculum, mastering classroom management, and trying to stretch every dollar of your modest salary. But somewhere around years five to ten, things begin to shift. Your paycheck grows. Maybe it's from step increases, a master's degree, coaching a sport, or picking up summer school. Whatever the cause, more money starts to come in—but that doesn't mean more peace of mind. This is when strategy must replace improvisation. The habits you form now will determine if this extra income works for you or just disappears.

It's easy to let lifestyle creep happen slowly. That second teaching job turns into a new car, nicer clothes, or a more expensive apartment. Maybe you finally feel like you "deserve" to take a vacation without guilt. And you do. But without a plan, higher income just gets absorbed. One of the biggest mistakes mid-career teachers make is increasing expenses at the same pace as their earnings. Before you know it, you feel just as broke as you did your first year. This is where budgeting transforms from basic tracking into strategic forecasting. Your budget should now reflect long-term goals, not just short-term survival.

At this stage, you should be asking bigger questions: Are you contributing to your 403(b) or 457(b)? Are you maxing out your Roth IRA? Are you saving for your children's education? Are you on track to buy a home or pay one off? Have you revisited your insurance policies or checked in with a financial advisor? With higher income comes a higher obligation to take ownership of your financial choices. Not because you're behind—but because you're building something that matters.

Mid-career is also when debt decisions come back into focus. Are you still paying off your student loans? Are you carrying credit card balances? If you have children, are you starting to feel the pressure of childcare or college savings? These years often require hard decisions. You may need to prioritize paying off high-interest debt over funding every other goal at once. This is when creating a financial hierarchy becomes crucial. You can't do everything at once, but you can make intentional progress in stages.

If you're in a dual-teacher household, your combined income might be the highest it's ever been. But that doesn't mean your strategy should be on autopilot. Coordinating benefits, maximizing retirement contributions, and managing joint expenses takes teamwork and communication. The same applies to single-income households or single teachers with children. The responsibilities are different, but the need for clarity and control is universal.

One of the greatest dangers during this phase is taking advice from other teachers without fully understanding their financial context. Colleagues may mean well, but everyone's circumstances are different. What worked for a teacher with no children and a working spouse may not work for you. This is when personalized advice matters most. Whether it's from a fee-only advisor, a financial coach, or your district's retirement consultant, get advice that's tailored to your actual life.

This is also the time to invest in your future self—and not just financially. Can you take professional development that leads to a salary bump? Could you start a side business or passion project that supplements your income? Do you need to build a stronger emergency fund to guard against burnout or a mid-year exit? Growing income is a tool, not a destination. Make sure you're using it to give yourself options.

Revisit your budget at least once a semester. Treat it like a living document. Adjust for changes in pay, healthcare premiums, childcare costs, or tuition bills. Don't let your finances drift just because your salary is finally comfortable. Comfort can lull you into complacency, and complacency is expensive.

Finally, use this phase to get honest about your long-term vision. What does financial independence look like for you? Do you plan to teach until full pension age? Do you want to retire early and do something else? Would you like to pay off your mortgage by 55 or take a sabbatical year? Your strategy should start aligning with the future you want—not just reacting to today's demands.

This part of your teaching journey is a gift. You're earning more, you know more, and you have more tools than when you started. Don't let the momentum go to waste. Sharpen your strategy and use these years to lay the financial foundation you'll build on for the rest of your life.

Chapter 12: Understanding and Maximizing Your 403(b), 457, and IRA Options

Let's begin with something that many teachers don't learn until late in their career—you have access to retirement savings vehicles that most of the public doesn't talk about at the dinner table. If you're lucky, someone in the teacher's lounge once mentioned a 403(b), or you saw a flyer about your district's 457 plan buried in a stack of HR paperwork. But odds are, no one ever sat you down and explained what these plans are, how they compare to traditional IRAs, or how to use them as the powerful financial tools they are. That's what this chapter is about: not just defining the acronyms, but empowering you to understand their purpose and build a strategy that aligns with your goals.

A 403(b) is similar to a 401(k), but it's designed specifically for employees of public schools, non-profits, and certain tax-exempt organizations. Contributions are made pre-tax, meaning they lower your taxable income today, and the investments grow tax-deferred until you withdraw the money in retirement. Think of it as a way to quietly invest in your future behind the scenes, paycheck by paycheck. A 457 plan, often offered alongside a 403(b), also lets you save pre-tax dollars, but with slightly different rules about withdrawals and catch-up contributions. The beauty of the 457? No early withdrawal penalty if you separate from service, which makes it a hidden gem for teachers considering a mid-career transition.

Then there are IRAs—Individual Retirement Accounts—which you open outside your school district. A traditional IRA works much like a 403(b), with pre-tax contributions and tax-deferred growth, though it comes with lower contribution limits. A Roth IRA, on the other hand, is funded with after-tax dollars, meaning you pay taxes now, but all your growth and withdrawals in retirement are tax-free. If you're a younger teacher, a Roth IRA can be especially powerful, allowing you decades of compounding tax-free. And if you're married to someone who has a higher income or works in the private sector, a Roth might complement your household's tax strategy in ways worth exploring.

So how do you choose? Start by looking at your current income, expected career trajectory, and retirement timeline. Are you early in your career and expecting raises and promotions? Roth options might be your best friend. Are you in a higher tax bracket now and planning to slow down in a few years? A traditional 403(b) could provide immediate tax relief. Many teachers assume they can only use one plan, but that's not the case. If you're able, you can contribute to both a 403(b) and a 457—potentially doubling your pre-tax savings. And you can often contribute to an IRA on top of those, depending on your income. This stacking strategy isn't just for the wealthy; it's for the informed.

Of course, contributing to a plan is just the beginning. Where you invest that money matters. Many teachers are steered toward annuities within their 403(b), especially in older plans managed by insurance companies. While annuities might offer guarantees, they also come with high fees and limited growth potential. Before you check a box or sign a form, ask to see your plan's investment menu. Look for low-cost index funds that track broad markets. If your 403(b) or 457 doesn't offer these options, consider lobbying your district or working with a financial advisor who understands the unique constraints of educator plans.

Let's also talk about the reality of cash flow. Contributing to retirement plans sounds noble, but when your paycheck barely covers rent, groceries, and student loans, how do you prioritize? This is where strategy trumps guilt. Start with your district match if available—never leave free money on the table. From there, consider the Roth IRA as your second stop, since it offers the most flexible long-term tax benefits. Only after maxing that should you revisit your 403(b) or 457, ideally choosing whichever offers better investment options and lower fees. It's not about doing everything at once. It's about creating a ladder and climbing it one rung at a time.

Mid-career teachers often hit a crossroads: they've been contributing for years but aren't sure if they're on track. This is when it's worth running a retirement projection. Many districts offer access to retirement calculators or advisors through their benefits portal. Take advantage of these. Plug in your years of service, current contributions, and projected retirement age. Then add in your pension (if you're vested) and social security eligibility. The goal isn't to create anxiety; it's to give you a roadmap. If the numbers don't align with your desired lifestyle, you've caught the gap early enough to course-correct.

For late-career teachers, maximizing catch-up contributions can be a game-changer. If you're over 50, both the 403(b) and the 457 allow you to contribute more than the standard limit. In some districts, these limits stack, giving you the opportunity to turbocharge your savings in your final working years. Don't assume it's too late. Every dollar saved now grows faster because it spends less time getting taxed and more time compounding. And if you're within a few years of retirement, consider dialing down your investment risk—but not eliminating it entirely. Inflation still matters in retirement, especially with rising healthcare costs.

Here's the kicker: most teachers don't get financial training as part of their credentialing. You weren't taught how to analyze mutual funds or read a prospectus. That's not a personal failing—it's a systemic one. So don't be afraid to ask questions. Talk to HR. Attend a retirement planning workshop. Meet with a fiduciary advisor who charges by the hour if that's more accessible. The more you demystify this part of your financial life, the more confident you'll feel. Retirement savings isn't about having a crystal ball. It's about knowing your options and using them wisely.

Your paycheck may never make headlines, but your decisions can still build wealth. A well-funded 403(b), a strategic Roth IRA, and a low-fee 457 plan can combine to offer you the freedom to retire with dignity and choices. Don't underestimate the impact of consistency. You're not trying to time the market—you're building a long-term habit. And while pensions are valuable, they don't always cover everything. Supplementing with your own savings gives you leverage. It lets you decide when you retire, not the district. It lets you travel, support your family, or even volunteer or consult if you choose. You're not just saving money. You're buying freedom. Make each contribution count.

Chapter 13: Catch-Up Contributions and Mid-Career Investing Moves

There is a unique kind of pressure that sets in around your 40s or early 50s—the sense that time is slipping faster than it used to. For teachers, that pressure often comes with the weight of knowing you've dedicated your career to shaping young minds while putting your own financial goals on hold. This chapter is about catching up—not just with investments, but with belief in yourself as a wealth-builder. Whether you're behind on retirement savings, still paying off student loans, or simply feeling overwhelmed by all the choices, this chapter will help you assess where you stand and how to move forward with purpose.

Let's start with the reality: many mid-career educators are under-saved. Maybe you took a break to raise children, had a partner out of work, or spent more than a decade surviving paycheck to paycheck. You are not alone. According to national data, a large percentage of public employees—including teachers—approach retirement with less than $100,000 saved outside of their pension. But here's the good news: there's still time. And there are specific tools and strategies designed to help you make up ground, including catch-up contributions, employer retirement plan adjustments, and strategic allocation changes that reflect your shortened investment timeline.

Catch-up contributions are the IRS's way of giving you a second wind. If you're age 50 or older, you're allowed to contribute more to retirement accounts like a 403(b), 457(b), or IRA than younger savers. As of 2025, you can contribute up to $23,000 in a 403(b) or 457(b), plus an additional $7,500 in catch-up contributions. That's $30,500 a year—per account. If you and your spouse are both teachers and eligible for both types of plans, you can potentially double that impact. Don't underestimate the compounding effect of these contributions, especially if you have 10-15 years left in your career.

Mid-career is also the time to take a hard look at your asset allocation. Are you overly conservative because of fear? Or too aggressive because you feel behind? Both extremes can hurt. A balanced portfolio—one that reflects your actual risk tolerance, time horizon, and goals—is key. Rebalancing doesn't mean day-trading or chasing the market. It means reviewing your investment mix annually, especially in light of life changes like divorce, inheritance, kids entering college, or job changes.

This is also the stage to consider Roth conversions or adding Roth options to your mix. If you expect your income to decline in retirement, converting some traditional 403(b) assets to a Roth IRA during your higher-earning years could offer long-term tax advantages. But it's not always the right move, especially if you're in a high tax bracket now. Talking to a financial planner or tax advisor about your specific scenario can clarify whether a partial conversion makes sense—or if it's better to prioritize maxing out your pre-tax options.

Let's talk strategy. If you're mid-career and behind, your savings rate matters more than your investment return. Set a target: can you save 20% of your income this year? If that feels impossible, try 10%. Then automate it. Use step-ups to increase your contribution by 1% each semester. These incremental moves matter. One often overlooked strategy is to time these increases with your district's pay raises or step increases. That way, the extra savings come out before you've adjusted to having more money in your checking account.

Your 40s and 50s also demand new conversations about risk. Do you have enough disability insurance? How long could you cover your mortgage if you lost your income tomorrow? Are you still the financial point person for extended family members who haven't gotten their finances together? All of these responsibilities can pull focus from your own planning. It's okay to acknowledge that. But it's also necessary to draw financial boundaries that allow you to save aggressively while protecting your mental health.

Another powerful tool is the 457(b), often available to public school teachers alongside the 403(b). Unlike the 403(b), a 457(b) plan doesn't penalize you for withdrawing funds before age 59½ if you separate from service. That flexibility makes it a great bridge account for teachers looking to retire early or transition to part-time work in their 50s. If your district offers both plans, consider contributing to both—especially once catch-up contributions become available.

Lastly, don't forget to review your pension estimates. Knowing your projected pension income helps you define your "gap number"—how much you'll need to supplement with personal savings. That clarity makes your goals feel more concrete. It's not about hitting a magic number like $1 million. It's about knowing how your pension, Social Security, and retirement accounts work together to fund the life you want. Mid-career planning is less about perfection and more about course correction.

You may not have started early, but you are starting now. And that matters more than anything else. The best time to plant a tree was 20 years ago. The second-best time is today. Catch-up investing is not about shame—it's about reclaiming your power, no matter where you're starting from. Teachers know how to play the long game. You've already done it in the classroom. Now it's time to apply that same patience, strategy, and care to your future.

Chapter 14: Managing Credit Cards, Student Loans, and Teacher-Specific Forgiveness Plans

Credit cards can either be a stepping stone to financial freedom or a trapdoor into debt—depending on how you use them. For many teachers, credit cards become a temporary crutch during summer months, unexpected classroom expenses, or emergencies that the paycheck can't quite cover. And while the flexibility they offer can feel like a lifesaver, interest rates can quietly wreak havoc if balances aren't paid off in full. Understanding how credit cards work is step one: interest compounds daily, minimum payments often barely chip away at the principal, and missed payments can sink your credit score fast. But they can also help build your credit history if you're strategic. Set automatic payments, never spend more than 30% of your credit limit, and avoid store cards that offer big promises and even bigger interest rates.

Student loans are a shadow that many teachers carry into the classroom, often with little guidance on how to manage them. For educators who went through graduate programs or teaching credential pathways, the debt can feel endless—especially when salaries don't reflect the level of education required. Federal loans offer flexibility, but you have to understand your repayment options: income-driven repayment plans (IDRs), Public Service Loan Forgiveness (PSLF), and Teacher Loan Forgiveness (TLF) are all on the table. But these programs don't work automatically—you have to jump through hoops, fill out the right forms annually, certify employment, and stay on top of deadlines. If you're not careful, you could miss out on thousands in forgiveness or end up making unnecessary payments.

Credit card debt and student loan debt feel different, but they affect your financial wellness in similar ways. Both chip away at your disposable income, both impact your credit score, and both can create stress that bleeds into your personal and professional life. The key difference is how you prioritize them. Credit card debt is typically higher-interest and should be paid off as aggressively as possible. Student loans—especially federal loans—may be more manageable and flexible, especially if you're eligible for forgiveness programs. This is where a teacher-specific financial strategy is critical. Knowing when to refinance, when to consolidate, and when to simply stay the course can save you tens of thousands over your career.

Let's talk about forgiveness. Public Service Loan Forgiveness has been the holy grail for many teachers—promising total loan cancellation after 10 years of payments while working for a qualifying employer. The problem? PSLF has historically had a poor approval rate, mostly because people weren't given the right instructions. But things have improved. If you're teaching full-time at a public school and have Direct Loans under an income-driven plan, you may qualify. And if you were previously denied, new rules and waiver periods may open the door again. Teacher Loan Forgiveness is different—it offers up to $17,500 in forgiveness after five years of consecutive teaching in a low-income school. It doesn't eliminate everything, but it's a strong start—especially if you don't plan on staying in the same district for a decade. Some teachers can actually qualify for both TLF and PSLF with the right planning.

Student loan consolidation and refinancing are tempting options, but they require caution. Consolidation through the federal government can simplify payments and help you qualify for forgiveness programs—but it may reset your progress if not done correctly. Refinancing with a private lender could get you a lower interest rate, but it disqualifies you from federal protections, forgiveness, and income-based repayment. Teachers, especially those who may qualify for PSLF, should tread carefully. A slightly lower interest rate isn't worth losing access to a program that could wipe your debt away entirely. The smartest move? Review your options with a nonprofit credit counselor or a fiduciary financial advisor who understands the teacher landscape. Not every loan servicer will give you unbiased advice.

Credit cards have their place—when used strategically. Consider opening a low-interest card with rewards that actually benefit your lifestyle. Travel rewards may not be relevant, but cash back on groceries, gas, or supplies can add up. Always pay more than the minimum, and avoid chasing sign-up bonuses if you're not sure you can pay off the balance. One card, paid consistently and used wisely, can help build your score. Multiple cards, used recklessly, can do lasting damage. Your credit score affects your ability to rent housing, buy a home, or even qualify for better auto insurance rates. Protect it like your teaching license—it matters more than most people think.

There are action steps every teacher can take right now. If you haven't already, check your credit report at AnnualCreditReport.com and review for errors. Enroll in autopay on your credit cards and loans to avoid missed payments. If you're overwhelmed with multiple payments, look into federal loan consolidation—but only after understanding how it will affect your forgiveness eligibility. Contact your loan servicer to confirm whether your loans qualify for PSLF or TLF. If they don't give you clear answers, escalate. Keep a paper trail. Save every email. Your financial future is too important to leave to chance.

It's worth stating clearly: there is no shame in having debt. Most teachers do. What matters is how you manage it, how you advocate for yourself, and how you keep learning. Every on-time payment is a step forward. Every conversation you have about money breaks down a wall of silence. And every dollar you put toward your future is a reminder that you deserve financial peace—even if no one taught you how to get there until now. Debt is not a moral failing. It's a financial fact. And you can work with it.

Sometimes, managing debt means making hard decisions. Maybe that means living with a roommate a few more years. Maybe it means holding off on a car upgrade, or saying no to a big vacation. But those sacrifices aren't forever. They're strategic. They buy you breathing room, momentum, and the chance to build something sustainable. Every time you choose financial stability over instant gratification, you're rewriting your money story. And the best part? That story can change at any time.

You don't need to have everything figured out today. But you do need a plan. A five-year roadmap. A set of guardrails. A system that fits your real life as a teacher—not just someone's idea of what financial responsibility should look like. The world didn't prepare you for this. But now, you're preparing yourself. And that's the most powerful lesson of all.

Start with what you can control. Tackle one credit card at a time. Revisit your student loan paperwork. Set a monthly reminder to review your forgiveness status. Don't be afraid to ask questions—even the basic ones. Don't be afraid to push back. Don't be afraid to demand clarity from systems that were never designed with teachers in mind. You're not just surviving—you're leading. And that leadership includes your finances, too.

Chapter 15: Emergency Funds and Cash Flow Management During Tough Months

The rhythm of a teacher's year isn't like that of most professionals. Summers often come without a paycheck. Winter breaks can bring unexpected expenses. Some teachers are paid over 10 months, others over 12, and some switch districts and find themselves with no paycheck in August at all. Managing cash flow isn't just about being good with money—it's about surviving the unique ups and downs of a career in education. If you've ever found yourself rationing groceries in July or swiping a credit card in December just to get through, you're not alone. Cash flow management for teachers is a financial literacy priority that deserves plain language and real-world tools.

Let's start with the emergency fund. You may have heard the standard advice: save three to six months of expenses. But for teachers, this isn't just for emergencies like a job loss or a car repair. Your emergency fund is also your paycheck buffer when school is out. Think of it as a cushion that smooths the rough patches between contracts or during summer months. The ideal fund should cover essential bills—rent or mortgage, groceries, transportation, insurance, and utilities—for a few months. If you get paid on a 10-month schedule, your summer survival plan is your emergency fund in disguise.

Start small if needed. Even $500 in a separate savings account is a beginning. Automate transfers each month if possible. Consider directing a portion of your paycheck into a high-yield savings account, one that isn't too easy to dip into. This is not the money you tap for concert tickets or classroom decor. It's your safety valve. Treat it like you would treat classroom instructional hours—with intention and respect. Build toward your goal gradually, and revisit the number annually as your expenses change.

For those navigating irregular pay schedules, a budget built on monthly averages can prevent chaos. If your income fluctuates (e.g., coaching stipends, tutoring gigs, or pay spread across fewer months), map out your entire year on paper or a spreadsheet. Divide your annual income by 12 to get a monthly average. Then create a budget based on that number, not the higher months when checks feel abundant. This keeps lifestyle inflation in check and gives you a plan that works in the leaner months too.

Some teachers open two checking accounts—one for bills and essentials, the other for flexible spending. If your district offers a 10-month pay schedule, you might set aside a fixed percentage of each paycheck into the second account, earmarked for summer. Think of it as "paying yourself forward." When July hits, that money feels like a gift from your past self. It's a practice in discipline and delayed gratification—skills you already use daily in your classroom.

Consider building a mini-fund specifically for common teacher-specific costs. This could include back-to-school supplies, union dues, classroom decorations, or out-of-pocket professional development. If these expenses sneak up on you every year, treat them like a quarterly bill. Set aside $20 or $50 per paycheck into a sinking fund, labeled clearly for those teacher extras. When the expenses come around, you won't feel blindsided—you'll feel prepared.

Debt and emergency funds can co-exist. Many teachers ask, "Should I pay off debt or build savings first?" The answer: do both, but start with at least one month of expenses in savings. Without a cushion, every unexpected bill becomes new debt. Think of your emergency fund as armor—it keeps your progress protected while you chip away at loans or credit cards. Once you have some savings, you can increase your debt payments with less risk of setback.

During tough months—like December, with holiday pressure, or August, with school startup costs—having a cash flow plan matters more than ever. This is the time to look at your calendar and anticipate expenses before they hit. Write out every known cost: holiday gifts, travel, back-to-school shopping, union dues, etc. Set mini-goals for those months. Could you put away $50 a month starting in September to prepare for the holidays? That's less stressful than trying to do it all from a single December paycheck.

Financial stress is amplified when it's tied to your passion. Teaching is more than a job—it's identity, it's community, it's legacy. So when money gets tight, it doesn't just feel like a budget issue. It feels like failure. Let that go. Money trouble doesn't mean you're irresponsible or weak. It means you're living in a system that often undervalues the very people who shape future generations. But with planning, intention, and a few steady practices, you can turn that tide.

You don't need to be perfect. You need to be consistent. That's the secret to managing cash flow as a teacher. Not luck. Not a second job (though sometimes that helps). Just clarity and habits, built over time. You already teach perseverance and patience every day. It's time to apply those same values to your own financial life—with grace, with strategy, and without shame.

Chapter 16: Buying a Home on a Teacher's Budget – What's Smart vs. What's Stretch

Buying a home is a milestone that often carries emotional weight. For teachers, it can feel like both a dream and a dilemma. You want a safe, comfortable place to live, perhaps with a yard or space for a home office, in a district where you feel proud to work and raise your kids. But as you scroll real estate listings, the numbers don't always seem to line up with your paycheck. The market doesn't care that you stay late grading papers or spend your own money on classroom supplies. Mortgage underwriters won't be impressed that your students made two years of reading growth. So how do you make it work? How do you buy a home that brings peace instead of pressure? This chapter is here to walk you through that answer.

Let's start by getting honest about the trade-offs. There's a difference between buying a home that stretches you and buying one that silently strangles you. Stretching might mean tightening your dining-out budget or holding off on new furniture. Strangling is when the mortgage leaves you no cushion for car repairs, medical bills, or even summer income gaps. One rule of thumb: your total housing payment—including mortgage, property taxes, and insurance—shouldn't exceed 28-30% of your gross monthly income. If you're pushing beyond that, pause. That's not ambition—that's stress on a payment plan. Teachers already live with enough invisible burdens. Your home shouldn't become another one.

Next, understand what lenders look for versus what actually works for your lifestyle. You might qualify for a larger loan than you can realistically manage. Lenders use debt-to-income ratios, but they don't account for irregular summer pay, extra classroom expenses, or tuition savings for your kids. A pre-approval letter is not a permission slip to spend recklessly. It's just a boundary of what a bank is willing to risk—not what your life can absorb. Consider creating your own budget-based approval number: calculate what you could comfortably spend on a monthly mortgage and reverse-engineer a purchase price from there.

Think about location not just in terms of where you want to live, but how far your dollar goes. In some districts, living close to your school might mean paying a premium for housing, while neighboring zip codes offer more space and affordability. That commute trade-off isn't just about gas and time—it's also about sanity. Can you tolerate a 25-minute drive if it means saving $300 a month? Or would being able to walk to work improve your quality of life enough to justify a higher price tag? There's no right answer here. It's about aligning the decision with your values, not someone else's version of success.

Now let's talk about timing. There's pressure to buy as soon as you feel "settled," but slow down. Do you have an emergency fund saved? Are you contributing to retirement? Have you tackled high-interest debt? Buying a home before addressing these priorities can backfire. You might be better off renting a little longer and strengthening your foundation. Remember, owning a home doesn't make you financially mature—being financially ready to own one does. A house isn't a badge of adulthood. It's a responsibility, and one that sticks around longer than some teaching jobs.

Teachers also have access to specific programs that can help. Look into teacher-specific grants, down payment assistance programs, and nonprofit housing initiatives. Organizations like the Good Neighbor Next Door program through HUD can offer discounted homes to teachers in certain areas. Don't just search Zillow—search city, county, and state housing programs for educators. Many of these opportunities aren't advertised widely, and it's worth making a few phone calls to local housing authorities or school HR reps who may know what's available.

Be honest about your emotional drivers. It's easy to fall in love with a kitchen or a neighborhood and ignore the price tag. But you have to live with the mortgage longer than the honeymoon phase of homeownership. Before you tour homes, write down your non-negotiables. What really matters to you: Walkable neighborhoods? A good school district for your kids? Space for caregiving an aging parent? These aren't just preferences—they're anchors that help you avoid being swept up in marketing and social pressure. Make your list before emotion clouds your judgment.

Be prepared for the true cost of homeownership. Your mortgage payment is just the beginning. Property taxes, homeowner's insurance, maintenance, repairs, HOA dues, and utility spikes in summer or winter all come with the territory. If you're moving from an apartment where your landlord handled repairs, brace yourself for the emotional and financial toll of the first broken water heater or roof leak. Build a "house buffer" fund into your savings—even if it's just $50 a month to start. Homeownership can be joyful, but only when it doesn't become a source of chronic worry.

Finally, don't compare your timeline to others. Some of your peers might buy houses in their 20s with family help. Others may rent until their 40s while building other forms of wealth. There is no universal scoreboard. Buying a home doesn't automatically mean you're winning. It simply means you've taken on a new set of responsibilities. The real flex? Being able to sleep at night knowing your bills are paid, your home is cared for, and you're not one unexpected expense away from panic.

The smartest home purchase is the one that leaves room in your life for living. That means budgeting for vacations, classroom supplies, and pizza Fridays. It means having bandwidth for joy and not just obligations. It means walking into your home at the end of a long school day and breathing a sigh of relief—not anxiety. If that means buying smaller, later, or differently than you expected, so be it. Your home should support your life, not swallow it.

Chapter 17: Insurance Checkup – Adjusting Coverage as Your Life Evolves

When you first started teaching, your life probably looked very different than it does today. Maybe you were living in a small apartment, had no kids, drove an older car, and your biggest financial worry was how to make your rent stretch until the next paycheck. Now, a few years or even decades later, things may be more complex. You might own a home, have children, carry a mortgage, support aging parents, or be thinking about retirement. With every shift in life comes a shift in risk. And with that, your insurance needs evolve. This chapter is about not just protecting your stuff, but protecting your peace of mind—and knowing what to keep, upgrade, or drop along the way.

Many teachers sign up for their insurance benefits once and never revisit them. It's understandable—you're busy, and the enrollment forms are often confusing. But failing to review your insurance annually is like leaving your lesson plans untouched for a decade. Life changes. A policy that made sense when you were 25 may be wildly insufficient at 45. Let's start with life insurance. If someone depends on your income—a spouse, child, or parent—you probably need term life insurance. Not through your school district alone, but a separate policy that follows you regardless of where you work. You can often get $500,000 or even $1 million in coverage for less than what you spend on your monthly streaming subscriptions. If you've recently had a baby or taken on more debt, your policy might need an upgrade.

Auto insurance is another area teachers often overlook. You might have chosen a bare-bones policy years ago to save money. But as your assets grow, you need to think beyond state minimums. If you cause an accident and are underinsured, your wages can be garnished. That's not just inconvenient—that's devastating. Review your liability limits. Do you have uninsured motorist protection? Do you know how your coverage works if you drive students in your personal car for extracurriculars? You need to. These are the kinds of risks that don't make headlines but wreck lives quietly. Protect yourself like your future depends on it—because it does.

Let's talk home insurance. If you own a home, your policy should reflect the actual cost to rebuild, not just what you paid for it. With construction costs rising, many homeowners are underinsured and don't know it. Make sure your policy includes extended replacement cost coverage and checks for water backup, mold, and other sneaky exclusions. If you rent, you still need renter's insurance. Your landlord's policy doesn't cover your personal belongings. And if you're a traveling teacher or working multiple schools, ask about portability.

Disability insurance might be the most overlooked protection in a teacher's financial toolkit. If you're a young, healthy educator, it's easy to assume you'll always be able to work. But one accident, diagnosis, or mental health crisis can change everything. Most schools offer basic short-term disability, but very few offer long-term coverage that lasts until retirement. You may need to supplement with a private policy, especially if you're the primary earner in your household. Think of it this way: Your ability to earn an income is your biggest asset. If it disappears, what happens to your mortgage, your kids' college fund, your retirement dreams?

As your life evolves, you may also need to consider umbrella insurance. This type of policy kicks in when your auto or home insurance reaches its limit, and it covers things like lawsuits and large claims. Let's say someone trips at your house during a school fundraiser. Or you accidentally post something online that someone deems defamatory. Your regular insurance might not be enough. An umbrella policy gives you an extra layer of protection for a relatively low annual cost.

Health insurance deserves its own attention. Many teachers stick with their district's default health plan without exploring alternatives. Are you overpaying for coverage you don't use? Are you under-covered for chronic conditions? If your district offers a Health Savings Account (HSA)-eligible plan, it might be worth switching, especially if you're healthy and want a tax-advantaged way to save for future medical expenses. And don't forget about dental and vision—routine neglect can lead to big, unexpected bills. Open enrollment is not a nuisance; it's an opportunity.

As you get older, long-term care insurance becomes relevant. If you're in your 40s or 50s, now is the time to explore it—before premiums become unaffordable or health disqualifies you. This is especially important if you don't have adult children who can care for you or if you're single. Nursing home and in-home care costs can easily exceed $100,000 a year. Planning ahead isn't morbid. It's mature.

So what does a true insurance checkup look like? Once a year—preferably before open enrollment season—you sit down and review every type of coverage you have. Print out your policies. Highlight what you don't understand. Schedule a meeting with your HR representative, a financial planner, or a trusted insurance agent. Ask yourself: If I died tomorrow, would my family be okay? If I got into an accident next week, would my policy actually pay out? If a tornado hit my house, could I rebuild? Don't wait until something happens to find out you were unprepared.

Insurance doesn't solve all financial problems. But it's the safety net under every plan you make. As a teacher, you've worked hard to build a stable life—you deserve to protect it. Taking the time to adjust your coverage isn't a luxury. It's a necessity. You can't control everything, but you can make smart, proactive choices that shield your future self from chaos. That's not fear-based planning—that's financial maturity. And it's one more way to practice the same care for yourself that you show your students every day.

Chapter 18: Estate Planning 101 – Wills, Powers of Attorney, and Guardianship

You've spent your life building something meaningful—not just in your classroom, but in your home, your family, your relationships, and your financial world. Estate planning is not about how much money you have. It's about ensuring that what you've built is protected, directed, and passed on with clarity and dignity. For teachers, who often live on modest but consistent salaries, estate planning is just as important as for anyone with a larger income. This chapter is about helping you understand the foundational tools—wills, powers of attorney, guardianship designations—and why they matter more than you think.

Many teachers assume that estate planning is something only wealthy people need. That's a dangerous misconception. If you have a family, own property, care for a child or a dependent parent, or simply want to have a say in what happens if you become incapacitated, you need an estate plan. This is especially true if you're part of a two-teacher household, raising children, or nearing retirement. The goal here is not to fear-monger—it's to equip. Because having a basic estate plan in place is not morbid; it's responsible.

Let's begin with wills. A will is your legal voice after you're gone. It names who gets what, how, and when. Without a will, the state decides for you—and those decisions may not reflect your values or wishes. As a teacher, maybe you want your niece to inherit your classroom library, or you want your partner—who isn't legally married to you—to receive your pension benefits. Those wishes don't count unless they're written down and legally binding. A will lets you speak clearly in the moments when your voice is needed most.

Next, powers of attorney. These come in two forms: financial and medical. A financial power of attorney allows someone you trust to make money decisions on your behalf if you're unable to. A medical power of attorney (or healthcare proxy) empowers a loved one to make health decisions when you can't. Imagine you're in a car accident, or hospitalized with a sudden illness. Who speaks for you? Who pays your bills? These are not just hypothetical questions—they're real, and the answers must be established in advance.

Guardianship designations matter immensely if you have children. If something happens to you and your spouse (or co-parent), who will care for your kids? If you don't designate someone in a will, the courts will choose—and that choice may be based on availability, not alignment with your parenting values. Guardianship documents allow you to name who you want, and who you don't want, to raise your children if you can't. It's one of the hardest conversations, but one of the most vital acts of love and planning you can make.

A common question teachers ask is, "Can I just write something down on paper and sign it?" The answer is: sometimes. A handwritten will (called a holographic will) is valid in some states, but not in others. Even where it's legal, it's often contested. The safer, wiser route is to use a legal template approved in your state or consult an attorney. Many teachers' unions or state retirement systems even offer free or low-cost legal services. It's worth looking into. Peace of mind has a price—and it might be more affordable than you think.

Some teachers also ask whether a trust is necessary. The short answer: it depends. A trust can help avoid probate (the court process of validating a will), keep your affairs private, and simplify inheritance. If you have a special needs child, a blended family, out-of-state property, or anticipate a longer retirement needing asset protection, a trust might make sense. But if your life is relatively straightforward and you have named beneficiaries on key accounts (like your 403(b), pension, or life insurance), a will may be sufficient. The key is to assess—not assume.

Don't overlook beneficiary designations. Your 403(b), 457, pension, life insurance, and even your bank accounts may have named beneficiaries. Those designations override your will. If your ex-spouse is still listed on your retirement plan, they will get the money—even if your will says otherwise. So do a beneficiary audit every few years or after major life events. This is one of the simplest but most overlooked ways to keep your estate plan aligned with your real life.

As your life evolves, revisit your documents. Marriage, divorce, having kids, buying a house, illness, aging parents, retirement—each milestone is a cue to check your plan. Estate planning isn't one-and-done. It's a living process. Keep your documents in a safe but accessible place, and make sure a trusted person knows how to find them. Don't just file them and forget them. Revisit. Review. Revise.

Ultimately, estate planning is an act of love, not wealth. It's not about control—it's about care. For yourself, your loved ones, and your values. Teachers know how to prepare their students for the future. This is how you prepare your family. It's how you ensure that your lessons—financial and otherwise—live on in the people and causes that matter most to you.

Chapter 19: Helping Your Kids Without Sacrificing Your Own Future

It's one of the most emotionally charged financial decisions a teacher can make—helping your children. Whether it's covering soccer fees, paying for college, co-signing a loan, or offering them a place to stay after graduation, the instinct to support our kids is often immediate and powerful. But that instinct, when left unchecked, can pull directly from your own stability. This chapter isn't about guilt-tripping you into saying "no" to your kids. It's about helping you say "yes" to your future without having to say "no" to theirs. You can support them thoughtfully, without draining your own retirement, losing sleep over debt, or sacrificing your long-term peace of mind. Let's walk through how.

Start with clarity, not emotion. Helping your kids can't just feel like the right thing—it needs to be a financially healthy thing. Before writing a check or volunteering to help with bills, pause and look at your own numbers. Have you funded your emergency savings? Are you on track with your pension or 403(b)? Do you have high-interest debt hanging over your head? Financial generosity is only generosity when it's sustainable. If you're giving from a place of depletion, you're not actually helping anyone—you're postponing a future crisis.

Educators often carry emotional burdens from their classrooms into their homes. You're used to solving problems, nurturing others, and stepping up when no one else will. It's part of who you are—and part of what makes this question so hard. But here's a shift worth embracing: your job is to model healthy financial boundaries for your kids, not just meet their short-term needs. A child who sees you protecting your retirement, making smart trade-offs, and living within your means learns more from your actions than from any allowance you might give them.

If your children are still young, start planning early and talking often. Open a 529 plan for their education if college is in the picture. Consider a custodial Roth IRA for teenage kids with earned income. Let them see the budgeting decisions you make, and invite them into low-stakes money conversations. "We're choosing not to eat out this week so we can save more for our trip this summer" teaches more than a hundred lectures on fiscal responsibility. And remember, the earlier you start these conversations, the more financial literacy becomes a family culture—not a one-time intervention.

For parents of older children, especially those heading into or already in college, the pressure ramps up. You want to protect them from debt, but you also can't bankrupt your future in the process. Explore options like having them apply for work-study jobs, consider in-state schools, and learn about the FAFSA and Pell Grant system. If they must borrow, teach them about subsidized versus unsubsidized loans, and why a degree with a reasonable ROI matters. Let them take on responsibility now so they're not overwhelmed later. You're not being selfish; you're teaching them how the real world works.

Mid-career teachers may also find themselves sandwiched—caught between helping adult children and supporting aging parents. It's a heavy place to stand. This is where boundary-setting becomes both a financial tool and an emotional lifeline. It's okay to say, "I can help, but here's what that looks like." Maybe it's a set monthly contribution, co-paying for a service rather than giving cash, or offering time instead of money. Define your line clearly—and revisit it often.

Sometimes the best support you can offer your kids isn't financial—it's structural. Help them build their own budgets. Point them toward credit education or financial literacy resources. Offer to review their job offers or walk them through setting up direct deposit and retirement contributions. You're empowering them, not enabling them. This shift from "how much can I give" to "how can I equip" is the difference between stress and sustainability—for both of you.

Be wary of emotional sabotage. Kids don't always mean to manipulate, but guilt has a way of sneaking into money conversations—especially when you've helped before. Set a precedent that financial decisions are made with intentionality, not on-the-spot pressure. Use phrases like "Let me look at my budget and get back to you" to buy time and avoid reactive giving. You're not just protecting your wallet—you're modeling self-respect and long-term thinking.

It's also worth looking at your current and future obligations. Are you still paying off your own student loans? Will helping your kids mean you can't max out your IRA this year? Do you plan to retire in the next decade? Every dollar that goes to someone else is a dollar not invested in your financial security. That doesn't mean you don't give—it just means you give from a place of awareness, not autopilot. Consider working with a financial advisor to model the impact of major financial decisions. You might be surprised at how quickly "small" gifts add up over time.

Finally, remember that legacy is more than money. What you teach your children by example—about boundaries, generosity, planning, and purpose—matters just as much as any check you write. Helping your kids succeed doesn't have to come at the cost of your future. With clear eyes and thoughtful planning, you can show them what real stewardship looks like—and i

Chapter 20: Helping Your Aging Parents – Caregiving, Money, and Emotional Boundaries

The role reversal that happens when teachers begin caring for their aging parents is rarely discussed in financial circles, yet it's one of the most emotionally and economically challenging periods in a person's life. If you're in this position, you're not alone. Thousands of educators juggle grading papers while managing doctor appointments for their parents, all while wondering how to afford assisted living or in-home care. This chapter isn't here to guilt you for not doing more or spending more—it's here to help you build a plan rooted in compassion, clarity, and boundaries. Because just like in the classroom, burnout is real—and when it comes to family, it can cost you far more than just your energy.

First, let's look at the actual costs. Long-term care is expensive. Whether it's home health aides, memory care, or skilled nursing, the costs can quickly climb into the thousands per month. If your parents haven't done any estate planning or long-term care insurance preparation, you may feel pressure to step in financially. But remember: stepping in emotionally does not mean emptying your savings. It means helping them review their resources—Social Security, pensions, Medicare, Medicaid eligibility, and even Veteran's benefits—before dipping into your own.

Have the uncomfortable conversations now. Ask if your parents have a will, healthcare proxy, power of attorney, and updated beneficiary forms. Too many teachers discover too late that their parent's affairs are a mess, with accounts inaccessible and decisions stalled. You don't need to be a lawyer to ask questions like, "If something happened to you, who would handle your bills?" or "Do you want to stay in this house if your health changes?" The sooner you start the conversation, the more prepared you'll be to help them maintain dignity without sacrificing your stability.

You may also need to decide how involved you're willing to be. Are you helping with transportation and phone calls, or are you on call 24/7 for emergencies? There's no shame in setting boundaries. If you're losing sleep, missing work, or draining your savings to support a parent who's unwilling to downsize or get help, it's okay to pause and reassess. Your role is to support—not to fix everything. A teacher who's burnt out at home can't show up fully in the classroom. Emotional boundaries are not selfish; they're strategic.

Financially, create a parallel track for planning: one for your parents, one for yourself. If your parent needs care, investigate Medicaid planning with an elder law attorney. Explore whether you or a sibling can be paid as a caregiver through state waiver programs. Document all expenses you cover—from prescriptions to home modifications. And whatever you do, don't co-sign debt for a parent unless you've fully explored the risks. If they default, your credit and peace of mind will suffer more than theirs.

Some teachers become the point person because they're "the responsible one." If you're managing all the bills and care alone, consider calling a family meeting or using an app to coordinate with siblings. Divide tasks like grocery runs, bill pay, or even rotating caregiving duties. If others can't help financially, they can still help logistically. Don't let guilt isolate you or convince you you're supposed to do it all. This is a marathon, not a sprint.

At the same time, don't lose sight of your own financial life. You still need to fund your retirement, update your own estate documents, and protect your income. That means prioritizing your emergency fund, maintaining disability insurance, and possibly revisiting your own healthcare options if caregiving starts to impact your hours or health. A teacher who sacrifices everything for others risks being left without a safety net themselves.

You may also need to prepare for hard decisions. What if your parent refuses care? What if you can't afford their preferred living arrangement? What if old family wounds resurface just as you're trying to coordinate hospice care? These aren't financial hypotheticals—they're real-world moments that require both heart and backbone. Your financial plan should include space for therapy, respite care, and even just a break. Caregiving is financial, emotional, and physical labor.

Lastly, recognize that you are doing enough. No spreadsheet, insurance policy, or trust fund can replace your love and presence. But neither should those things be absent. You can love deeply and still protect your own future. You can give generously and still say "no" when your savings are at risk. Helping your parents through this season is an act of grace—but so is helping yourself thrive beyond it.

This chapter is not about perfection. It's about preparing, prioritizing, and protecting everyone involved—including you. Because you matter in this equation, too.

Part III: Life as a Teacher – Relationships, Family, and Financial Boundaries

This section explores the deeply personal intersection between a teacher's finances and their most meaningful relationships—with children, partners, aging parents, and even themselves. It goes beyond the numbers and dives into the realities of living on a teacher's salary while trying to honor emotional commitments and cultural expectations. Here, we confront the pressure to help everyone you love—without losing your own financial footing.

Teachers are natural caregivers, and that instinct often spills outside the classroom—into parenting, caregiving, and community roles. But financial stability requires boundaries, not just generosity. These chapters walk readers through the hard conversations: how to support a child through college without wrecking your retirement, how to say "yes" to your parents without saying "no" to your own health and goals, and how to manage shared finances in a relationship where one or both partners teach.

We also look at legal and logistical necessities that often get put off—wills, guardianship, powers of attorney—making sure readers understand the power and protection that estate planning can offer their loved ones. In a profession that rarely slows down, this part encourages teachers to pause, assess, and realign their financial lives so they can care with clarity, not chaos.

By the end of this section, the reader will feel equipped to make thoughtful financial decisions within their relationships—without guilt, without overwhelm, and with the confidence to protect their future while still showing up for the people they love.

Chapter 21: Two Teachers, One Household – Coordinating Income, Benefits, and Retirement

When two teachers share a household, it can feel like a financial advantage at first glance. You understand each other's schedules, salary structures, and professional pressures. But even though the shared experience can foster emotional unity, managing finances between two educators comes with its own complexity. Teacher salaries are rarely high, but with the right strategy, two can indeed live better than one. Still, coordination is key. Income, benefits, taxes, retirement accounts, and career timing must be managed deliberately to build financial stability together.

Start with the income conversation. It may sound simple—combine the paychecks and budget accordingly—but in reality, it requires clarity about after-tax income, deductions, and any other sources of pay like coaching stipends, summer school, or tutoring. Many teachers are paid on different schedules (monthly vs. biweekly) and contribute to different benefit packages. It's important to lay out exactly what is coming in and when, then line it up with your household expenses. If one partner has a more consistent paycheck or better benefits, that needs to be factored into your shared strategy.

Health insurance is a major decision in two-teacher households. You may each have the option of enrolling in separate plans through your own district or combining coverage under one partner's plan. This is not just a math problem; it's also a logistics and lifestyle question. Which plan offers broader coverage? Which has the more manageable deductible or lower out-of-pocket max? Does your district offer incentives for spouses waiving coverage? Run the numbers annually and don't assume that staying in separate plans is automatically cheaper or easier.

Retirement planning is where many dual-teacher couples make critical mistakes. School systems often offer pensions, 403(b)s, 457(b)s, and sometimes Roth IRA contribution opportunities. But it's easy to assume that "we're both in the pension system" is enough planning. It's not. Each partner should know their pension vesting schedule, projected payout, and how their years of service and final average salary will be calculated. You should also coordinate voluntary savings: is one of you maxing out a 403(b) while the other contributes to a Roth IRA? Are both of you missing out on matching opportunities or catch-up contributions?

Debt repayment is another conversation that requires alignment. Are you each carrying student loan debt? Are your loans under PSLF? What about car payments, credit card balances, or medical debt? The way you repay as a couple should take into account tax filing status, interest rates, and your timeline for other goals like buying a house or having kids. One of the most effective things you can do is assign debt strategically—perhaps the lower-interest debt is tackled more slowly while you aggressively pay down the higher-interest items. Communication, again, is everything.

Then there are taxes. Filing jointly often makes sense for two teachers, but not always. If one of you has a side hustle or significant deductions, it might be worth evaluating whether married filing separately could create benefits. Look at what credits or deductions phase out based on joint income. Also understand how your state taxes your income and retirement contributions. Not all tax preparers are familiar with the intricacies of educator-specific deductions like out-of-pocket classroom spending or union dues, so make sure you're working with someone who knows the terrain.

Budgeting for a dual-teacher household can be empowering, but it requires mutual transparency and regular check-ins. Build a zero-based or values-based budget that accounts for savings, giving, living expenses, and lifestyle.

This includes small but essential line items: classroom supplies, travel for professional development, gifts for students, and summer income planning. If one of you earns significantly more due to longevity or extra duties, be honest about how that income will be allocated. Equality doesn't always mean 50/50—it means fair, based on your family's needs and values.

You'll also want to coordinate your timelines for retirement. It may sound far off, but decisions you make now will affect how, when, and where you can retire. Will one of you work longer for better benefits while the other transitions out? Will you retire at the same time to travel or care for grandkids? These questions impact not just pensions but also healthcare coverage, Social Security strategies (if applicable), and investment withdrawals.

One major mistake to avoid is assuming your spouse's benefits mirror your own. Even if you work in the same district, the fine print can differ. Pension formulas, leave accrual, and vesting rules may vary by start date or contract. It's vital to review each partner's retirement projections and HR documents individually, then coordinate from there. Make appointments with your district benefits specialist together and keep a shared folder of all documents.

Lastly, talk about what happens in the event of disability or death. Does each of you have adequate life insurance and long-term disability coverage? Have you named each other as beneficiaries? Do you have updated wills and powers of attorney? It's not morbid—it's responsible. Coordinating your finances as two teachers means protecting each other as well as planning together. As your lives evolve, so should your financial strategy—but always in sync, always informed, and always rooted in shared values and goals.

Chapter 22: Single and Teaching – How to Build a Strong Financial Foundation Solo

There's a unique strength that comes with managing your financial life solo, but it can also feel like a heavy weight. When you're the only one bringing home a paycheck, every decision—big or small—sits on your shoulders. Many single teachers know the feeling of watching colleagues split expenses with a spouse while they cover the rent, utilities, groceries, and emergencies alone. This chapter is about building a financial life that doesn't rely on anyone else, yet still leaves room for joy, security, and long-term peace. If you're teaching full-time, working side gigs, or just trying to stay afloat, you deserve a financial strategy that honors your effort and gives you room to breathe.

Let's begin by reframing the narrative: being single is not a disadvantage in money management—it's a different blueprint. You have more control over your spending priorities, fewer compromises, and the ability to act fast when you want to make changes. But you also need a cushion. Emergency funds become non-negotiable when you're the only income source. A car repair, a medical bill, or even a short-term disability can destabilize your entire budget. So one of the first solo strategies is setting a goal of saving at least three to six months' worth of living expenses, even if you build it slowly, $100 at a time.

Budgeting as a single teacher requires honesty and clarity more than perfection. There's no shame in spending on things that bring joy—whether that's a gym membership, books, or the occasional DoorDash after a long day. But each dollar has to be assigned with intention. One helpful strategy is the 50/30/20 method: spend 50% of your take-home pay on needs, 30% on wants, and 20% on savings or debt payoff. It's a guide, not a rulebook. If student loans or rent push your "needs" category up to 60%, then adjust accordingly—but make sure you're still prioritizing future-you with some consistent savings.

When it comes to retirement planning, single teachers must be extra proactive. You can't count on a spouse's pension, 401(k), or Social Security credits to supplement your own. That means maxing out your own 403(b), contributing to a Roth IRA if you qualify, and understanding your pension plan details like vesting, service credits, and projected payout. This is especially important if you've worked in multiple districts or taken time off. Don't leave money on the table just because HR never mentioned it clearly.

Insurance can also be an overlooked area for single educators. You may not think you need life insurance if no one relies on your income, but consider this: who would pay for your funeral or medical bills if something happened? A term policy that covers your final expenses and debts is often affordable and worth it. More importantly, disability insurance is essential. If you couldn't work for three months due to injury or illness, how would you pay your bills? Check if your district offers it, and if not, consider a private policy.

Social connection can impact your finances in unexpected ways. As a single person, you may feel more pressure to say yes to social plans, travel, or family obligations—especially if others assume you have more "disposable" income. This is where boundaries matter. It's okay to say, "That's not in my budget this month," or to offer alternative plans. Your future self will thank you for protecting your long-term goals over short-term expectations.

Housing is another key consideration. Renting may offer flexibility, but homeownership can provide long-term stability and equity—especially if you plan to stay in one place. However, buying solo means you need to be extra cautious: get preapproved, stay well within your budget, factor in maintenance costs, and have an emergency fund before closing. Don't let the pressure to "buy now" override the importance of buying smart.

Building wealth as a single teacher often requires creativity. You might explore tutoring, summer teaching, freelance curriculum writing, or even real estate. Every extra dollar you earn can be directed toward your goals. But be careful not to burn out. Time is a non-renewable resource. Be honest about what's sustainable, and make sure your side hustle supports—not sabotages—your health and mission as an educator.

Finally, don't wait to build your financial support system. Just because you're single doesn't mean you're alone. Find a trusted financial advisor, a tax pro, and an accountability partner who respects your goals and your values. Having people in your corner can help you make more confident decisions, ask smarter questions, and navigate complex systems. And it can make this whole money thing feel a little less lonely.

Living well and saving wisely as a single teacher is absolutely possible. It's not about doing everything perfectly. It's about building systems that support you, prioritizing your peace, and knowing that you have the power to write a financial story that reflects your strength—not your relationship status.

Chapter 23: Single Teachers With Kids – Planning, Priorities, and Peace of Mind

Being a single parent is a challenge no matter your profession, but for teachers, the pressure comes from all angles—low pay, long hours, emotional labor, and the constant feeling that both your students and your own children need more than you can give. Financial planning in this context isn't just about numbers on a spreadsheet; it's about making every dollar work for your household, protecting your peace, and building a future that doesn't leave you burned out or behind. This chapter is about giving you tools to think through that reality with intention.

Let's begin by acknowledging what many single teachers don't hear enough: you're doing an extraordinary job. You're keeping classrooms afloat while also managing dentist appointments, school pickups, and grocery lists. You are the breadwinner and the homework helper. You are it. Which means your financial plan has to do double duty. You can't afford guesswork or guilt-based budgeting. You need clarity, prioritization, and a system that supports your real life, not some idealized version of it.

Start with your base expenses. What are your fixed costs every month? Rent or mortgage, childcare, food, insurance, and utilities. Get honest about what you need to survive, and what you've been stretching to cover. Then identify your financial pressure points. Is your rent too high? Is childcare taking up 40% of your take-home pay? Is student debt crowding out room to save? Naming the source of stress is the first step to relieving it—and often, there are more options than you think.

For many single teachers, childcare is the single biggest expense after housing. If your district offers before- or after-school care with a teacher discount, use it. If you have family nearby, don't be afraid to ask for regular help—not as a favor, but as a system. Consider flexible summer programs that align with your calendar. The goal isn't to patch together survival month by month, but to create predictability and breathing room. That stability helps not only your wallet, but your mental health too.

Next, build a three-tier savings strategy. Tier one is your emergency fund—aim for $500 to $1,000 if you're just starting. That's your car repair, your sudden field trip fee, your buffer. Tier two is short-term needs: school clothes, holidays, summer gaps in pay. Tier three is long-term: your Roth IRA or 403(b). Even $25 a month matters. Consistency builds muscle. When you automate savings, you remove the guilt loop of "should I or shouldn't I?" and start acting in alignment with your future.

Let's talk debt. If you have student loans, check if you qualify for Teacher Loan Forgiveness or Public Service Loan Forgiveness (PSLF). Many single teachers don't realize that their years of service may already count. Call your loan servicer. Ask for a full account review. If you're on an income-driven repayment plan, your monthly payment may already be calculated based on your family size and income—but it needs to be recertified annually. Put a reminder in your phone each year during open enrollment.

One of the hardest conversations single parents have to have with themselves is about their children's college. Here's the truth: you can borrow for college, but you can't borrow for retirement. Set boundaries around what you can afford, and don't anchor your worth to how much you can contribute to a 529 plan. If you can do $25 a month, do that. But know that your child will benefit far more from watching you build a strong, secure financial foundation than from having an untouched savings plan that came at your own expense.

Don't skip insurance. Life insurance and disability insurance are crucial when your kids rely on you as the sole provider. A term life insurance policy is usually affordable—look for coverage that equals at least 6-10 times your annual income. And make sure you've named a legal guardian for your kids, along with a financial trustee. These aren't just estate planning steps; they're peace-of-mind steps. They ensure your children are protected no matter what.

Lastly, give yourself permission to ask for help. Whether it's through a local financial counselor, a friend who understands budgeting, or your HR department explaining benefits, you don't have to do this alone. The strongest financial plans aren't built in isolation—they're built through community, clarity, and choices made with love and foresight. You're already doing the hard work. Now it's time to make sure that work is building the life you and your children deserve.

Chapter 24: Saying Yes With Your Heart, But No With Your Wallet – Avoiding Financial Guilt

Teaching is a profession rooted in heart. Every day, you give more than what your contract stipulates—more time, more care, more of yourself. So it's no surprise that this same impulse to give shows up outside the classroom too. Whether it's donating to every student fundraiser, paying for classroom supplies from your own pocket, or helping out a family member who's hit a rough patch, your generosity is a reflection of your values. But here's the truth that often goes unsaid: just because you care deeply doesn't mean you can afford to give financially every time. And learning to say "no" with your wallet—while still saying "yes" with your heart—is one of the most important financial lessons any teacher can learn.

Financial guilt is real. It's especially real in service professions like education, where the emotional payoff of helping others is often used to justify underpayment. You may feel guilty turning down a student's request for supplies or saying no to a colleague collecting donations. But here's the thing: if every financial "yes" chips away at your own security, you're not helping anyone in the long term. Teachers deserve to retire comfortably, to live without debt, to have emergency savings, and to build a financial life that reflects their worth—not just their work ethic. Guilt shouldn't be your budget manager. Strategy should be.

Start by drawing a line between generosity and obligation. There is no shame in saying, "I can't contribute right now." Practicing financial boundaries doesn't make you selfish; it makes you sustainable. Consider setting an annual "giving" budget—an actual line item in your spreadsheet or budget app. Allocate a certain amount you feel comfortable donating or giving freely over the course of the year. That way, when requests come in, you have a plan. You can say, "I've already planned my giving for the year, but I wish you the best." It's not a cop-out. It's a boundary backed by intention.

Another root of financial guilt comes from family expectations—especially if you're the first in your family to have a stable job or pension. If you're seen as the "successful one," relatives may lean on you more than they should. And because you love them, you want to help. But supporting others financially at the cost of your own future isn't noble; it's dangerous. If you run out of resources in retirement because you were constantly helping everyone else, who's going to help you? Family support should never be a one-way street. Set expectations early and revisit them often.

There is also the guilt of comparison—the feeling that if another teacher can afford private school for their child, why can't you? Or if a friend is going on vacation every break, should you be doing the same? Social media only magnifies this pressure. But comparison is the thief of both joy and financial stability. You have no idea what debts, inheritances, or financial help others may be receiving behind the scenes. Run your own race. Measure your decisions against your values, not someone else's highlight reel.

Educators are often wired to put others first, so even basic financial self-care can feel indulgent. But it isn't. Putting money in your emergency fund is not selfish. Saying no to a loan request from a cousin is not cruel. Choosing not to buy another round of school supplies is not heartless. These are acts of financial self-preservation. They are how you make sure you can continue showing up for your students, your family, and your future self without burning out or breaking down.

If you're still working through this, here are a few practical scripts you can keep in your pocket:

- "I wish I could help right now, but it's not in my budget."
- "We have a set amount for giving this year, and we've already committed

it."

- "I have to focus on some personal financial goals right now, but I hope the fundraiser goes well."
- These responses are honest, kind, and rooted in the truth that you cannot give what you don't have.

If you feel guilty for saying no, ask yourself: am I actually responsible for this outcome? Am I being asked to fill a systemic gap with my personal money? Teachers are already underpaid and overextended—you should not be footing the bill for school supplies that your district should be covering or for needs that require broader community support. Your compassion is commendable, but your savings account is not a grant fund. Let that truth take root.

Finally, remember that financial boundaries aren't brick walls. They're gates you can open with intention. You can still be generous. You can still support your students, your school, and your community. But you can do it with clarity, without resentment, and without derailing your future. Let your heart lead, yes. But let your budget have a vote too. There's no guilt in that—only wisdom.

The next time you're tempted to give beyond your means, pause and ask: what am I saying no to in my own life when I say yes here? That simple question can recalibrate everything—and help you move forward with both purpose and peace.

Chapter 25: Boundaries With Family, Colleagues, and Friends Around Money

You became a teacher because you wanted to give. Maybe you were inspired by a great educator in your life. Maybe you wanted to make school feel safer than it felt for you. Maybe you felt called to uplift young people. Regardless of what brought you into this profession, the truth is that teaching is a giving career—of your time, your energy, your heart. But being a giver can blur lines. It can become hard to separate generosity from financial self-sacrifice, especially when the people you're trying to help are family, friends, or even coworkers who seem to be struggling too. This chapter is about creating healthy, sustainable boundaries around money, so that your giving doesn't come at the cost of your own peace or long-term financial security.

Family, especially parents and siblings, can be the most complicated terrain when it comes to financial boundaries. Maybe your parents supported you during your teaching credential process, and now you feel obligated to send money home. Maybe a sibling is constantly in a tight spot and turns to you for help, assuming your "stable job" means you can afford it. But you need to remember: your paycheck is not a family bailout fund. You are allowed to prioritize your own rent, health insurance, emergency savings, and retirement planning. Love doesn't require a wire transfer. If the roles were reversed, you'd want your loved ones to build their future too.

Colleagues can create tricky dynamics too, especially when money talk enters the breakroom. If you're at a school where some teachers are married to higher earners, they might not flinch at contributing $40 for every birthday or $20 for every baby shower. But that doesn't mean you have to match them. Say no gracefully. Say, "Not this time, but I'll contribute next round." Or bring a thoughtful card instead. Financial peer pressure exists even among teachers, and opting out is not a betrayal—it's a boundary.

One of the hardest things about boundaries is that people often don't like them. They may push back, guilt-trip, or act distant when you decline to lend money or split a vacation cost. But just like classroom management, consistency is key. When you clearly communicate your limits—and stick to them—people eventually adjust. If someone truly values your relationship, they'll learn to respect your no. And if they don't, that's revealing too.

Setting boundaries with adult children, nieces, nephews, or godchildren is its own category of emotional complexity. You may want to give them what you didn't have growing up—braces, camp fees, a laptop for college. But giving out of guilt or comparison to other families can quickly become financial self-sabotage. Ask yourself: Am I helping from a place of strength, or from a place of pressure? Your job as an adult isn't to make up for everyone else's choices. It's to model healthy ones.

Guilt is one of the most potent financial forces for teachers. You see what your students go through. You see how little your colleagues make. You remember your own upbringing. It can feel impossible not to give when you have even a little to offer. But your worth as a teacher, friend, or family member is not tied to your giving. Sometimes, the most loving thing you can say is: "I can't help financially right now, but I can help you think through a plan."

Boundaries aren't just about saying no; they're about saying yes to what actually matters. When you protect your budget, you protect your peace. When you say no to spontaneous spending, you're saying yes to your Roth IRA. When you decline to fund a cousin's last-minute crisis, you're saying yes to being able to retire one day without fear. Boundaries build your future. They don't weaken your relationships—they clarify them.

If you're new to setting financial boundaries, start small. Identify one area where you feel overextended. Maybe you're always picking up the tab at brunch, or contributing to every school fundraiser. This month, pick one to skip. Script your response ahead of time. You might say, "I'm working on some savings goals this semester, so I can't contribute right now." It doesn't need to be an apology. It's a statement of financial self-respect.

Another helpful strategy is to pre-plan your giving. Decide in advance what you can afford to give to others each month—whether it's $50, $100, or $0. When requests come in, you already know your number. It shifts the conversation from reactive to intentional. And if someone says, "But it's just $20," you can honestly respond, "That's outside my giving budget this month."

Boundaries are not walls; they're filters. They let the good in and keep the draining out. They allow you to be generous without being emptied. As a teacher, you already give more than most people will ever understand. Financial boundaries simply ensure that you can keep giving—sustainably, joyfully, and without resentment—for the long haul.

Chapter 26: Side Hustles and Summer Jobs – Pros, Cons, and Tax Implications

For many teachers, the school year ends, but the bills don't. The rhythm of a teacher's calendar often includes a long summer break that looks restful from the outside but can come with financial anxiety behind the scenes. Whether it's picking up a summer job, tutoring on the side, or diving into a passion project that pays, educators are no strangers to the hustle. But what often goes unspoken is how to make those extra income streams work *for* you—not just tire you out further. The goal of this chapter is to unpack not only the emotional and physical costs of side work, but also the financial implications, tax realities, and strategic ways to build a side income without losing sight of why you became a teacher in the first place.

Let's start with the pros. Side hustles and summer jobs can provide breathing room, help chip away at debt, or fund goals like homeownership, family vacations, or emergency savings. They offer a form of agency, allowing teachers to supplement often stagnant salaries without waiting on district raises or contract renegotiations. For some, these gigs become creative outlets—teaching yoga, baking, starting Etsy shops—that reconnect them with forgotten parts of their identity. For others, summer camps, curriculum consulting, or test-prep gigs keep them connected to the education world while earning extra pay. These are valid, honorable ways to stretch a salary and reclaim some financial control.

Now, the cons. The mental and physical toll of extra work is real. Teachers already operate in high-stress environments with long hours. Adding more commitments can burn the candle at both ends, leading to exhaustion, burnout, and in some cases, health consequences that no paycheck can justify. There's also the hidden cost of time away from family, missed rest, and the risk of neglecting long-term goals in favor of short-term gains. Without intentional planning, side hustles can become band-aids for larger structural problems in your financial life. You don't want to work 60+ hours a week year-round just to feel like you're barely treading water.

One of the biggest misunderstandings about side work is how it affects your taxes. Many educators assume that because they're "just making a little extra money," the tax rules are relaxed. They're not. Any money you earn from a side hustle, whether tutoring, selling goods, or freelancing, is considered taxable income by the IRS. If you're paid more than $600 by any one client or platform, you'll likely receive a 1099 form. But even if you don't, the IRS still expects you to report the income. Teachers must understand self-employment tax, potential quarterly estimated payments, and the deductions you may qualify for to reduce your taxable income.

Speaking of deductions, side hustles come with new opportunities—and responsibilities. If you're earning income as an independent contractor or freelancer, you can deduct legitimate business expenses: mileage, supplies, internet costs, software, home office space, and more. But these deductions require documentation. That means keeping receipts, tracking expenses, and maintaining separate accounts if possible. Mixing personal and business finances can complicate things quickly. The key is to treat even your small-scale hustle like a small business. Not in terms of pressure, but in terms of structure.

Some teachers wonder whether forming a business entity like an LLC is necessary. In most cases, it's not required for small side gigs. But there are reasons to consider it if your income is growing. An LLC can provide limited liability protection and open the door to more formal business operations. It may also enhance credibility if you're working with clients. However, LLCs come with administrative responsibilities and state fees. For many educators, operating as a sole proprietor with well-kept records and basic tax planning is sufficient. If you do decide to formalize, consult a tax professional or attorney who understands both education and small business laws.

It's also worth discussing how side income interacts with student loan repayment and benefits. If you're on an income-driven repayment plan, additional income could increase your payment. If you're pursuing Public Service Loan Forgiveness (PSLF), side income does not disqualify you as long as your *main* employment remains full-time at a qualifying organization. But it may change your Adjusted Gross Income (AGI), which is used to calculate payment amounts. Make sure you understand how your earnings are reported and how they affect the rest of your financial picture. Don't let a side hustle accidentally slow your long-term debt strategy.

Here's where planning comes in. If you choose to pursue a side hustle or summer job, have a purpose for the money. Create a short-term goal: pay off a credit card, build a $5,000 emergency fund, or save for classroom supplies without putting it on your own dime. Designate a specific account for this money, and keep it separate from your regular paycheck. This reinforces your sense of progress and helps prevent the dreaded "Where did it all go?" feeling. More than that, it protects your peace. Your time is valuable. Make sure it's producing results, not just revenue.

Also, give yourself permission to say no. Just because you *can* take on a side gig doesn't mean you have to. Your well-being is part of your wealth. If summer break is your only time to rest, recuperate, or travel, that is just as valid as working. You are not failing financially if you choose not to monetize every free hour. What matters most is that your decisions align with your values, your current needs, and your long-term goals. There is no single right answer—only what works for your real life.

In the end, side hustles can be a powerful tool or a silent trap. The difference is in how intentionally they're used. For teachers, who are used to doing more with less, the temptation to keep adding "just one more thing" is always present. But your time and energy are not infinite. Be strategic. Be clear about your why. Understand your tax obligations, document your deductions, and protect your time. Most importantly, remember that financial literacy isn't about constantly working more—it's about making smarter, more informed decisions with what you already have.

Chapter 27: Don't Just Listen to the Lounge – Why Peer Financial Advice Can Derail You

The teacher's lounge is a space of solidarity, laughter, and sometimes even therapy. But when it comes to money, it can also become a chamber of misinformation. One teacher may proudly proclaim they're taking a loan against their pension to pay off credit cards, while another swears by putting everything on a rewards credit card because they "always pay it off." As a teacher, it's easy to assume advice from peers is trustworthy because you share similar financial constraints. But shared experience doesn't always mean shared expertise. Financial decisions should be grounded in facts, not anecdotes, no matter how confident or persuasive they sound at the copy machine.

Peer advice often comes from a place of good intentions—but good intentions can still steer you wrong. Most people don't share the full picture when talking about money. A colleague who says they're maxing out their 403(b) may not mention the debt they're quietly juggling or the spousal income that cushions their budget. What's presented as financial wisdom might be specific to their household, their goals, or even their blind spots. Without context, imitating someone else's choices is like teaching from someone else's lesson plan without knowing the learning standards—it may look fine on the surface but miss the mark entirely for your needs.

Teachers often trust one another because of the shared emotional labor and camaraderie of the job. But that emotional closeness can blur the lines between friendly support and sound guidance. For example, if a fellow teacher urges you to skip buying disability insurance because they "never got hurt," it might feel dismissive to push back. But your finances aren't something to gamble with just because a coworker rolled the dice and didn't lose. Their luck isn't your security. Financial literacy means learning when to say, "I'm happy that worked for you, but I'm going to make a more informed decision."

Social proof is powerful. If five teachers in the lounge are all telling you to refinance your student loans with a private lender, it's natural to feel like you're missing out if you don't. But this herd mentality can lead to serious mistakes. Private refinancing often eliminates access to Public Service Loan Forgiveness (PSLF)—a benefit specifically designed for public educators. Once you're out of the federal system, you can't go back. That's not just a minor consequence; it could mean the difference between tens of thousands of dollars in forgiveness and a debt load that never lightens.

It's not just big decisions that peer advice can complicate. Even casual talk about budgeting, summer jobs, or investing can get distorted by ego, fear, or misinformation. One teacher might say they "don't believe in credit scores" and have "never had a problem," while another might brag about cashing out their 403(b) early to buy a car. These comments may sound confident, but they often mask deeper financial instability. Don't let someone else's highlight reel shape your real-life choices. Ask yourself: what's their source? What's the full story? And most importantly, does their advice align with your goals?

One way to gently break away from lounge talk is to reframe it. Instead of engaging in financial one-upmanship, turn the conversation toward curiosity. Try asking, "How did you learn about that option?" or "What made you decide to go that route?" These questions shift the focus from performance to process. They also buy you time to gather facts before making decisions. This isn't about being dismissive—it's about being discerning. You can respect someone's experience without replicating their choices.

Financial advice should be specific to your situation—your salary, your debt, your retirement plan, your goals. That means turning to professionals who understand educator pay structures, pensions, and benefits—not just someone who read a finance blog once. You don't need to become an expert overnight, but you do need to build a reliable circle of information. That might include your district's HR representative, a fee-only financial planner who works with public sector clients, or even nonprofit organizations that serve teachers. A solid plan is rooted in real expertise, not hallway hearsay.

That said, don't feel guilty if you've made decisions based on peer advice in the past. We all do what we can with the information we have. Financial literacy is a journey, and realizing that not all sources are equal is part of the process. What matters most is that you start asking better questions now. Start checking the source. Start evaluating what's being said—and what's being left unsaid. It's not disloyal to your colleagues to do what's best for your own future.

There's something deeply affirming about hearing, "me too" in a staff lounge. But when it comes to money, "me too" can quickly turn into "me, too late." Trust your instincts when something feels off. Ask for more than just reassurance—ask for information, for data, for clarity. Seek out the tools and voices that make you feel stronger, not just seen. That's what real financial community looks like.

The lounge will always be there—for laughs, for venting, for survival. But when it comes to your finances, step outside of it. Your future deserves more than word-of-mouth wisdom. It deserves depth, truth, and the kind of guidance that helps you thrive—not just get through the week.

Chapter 28: How to Interview a Financial Advisor – 25 Questions Every Teacher Should Ask

Finding the right financial advisor can feel as intimidating as trying to teach a new subject outside your certification. You know you need help, but you're not always sure how to ask the right questions—or even what those questions should be. As a teacher, you're already underpaid and overstretched, which means every dollar and every piece of advice matters. The right advisor can help you retire with dignity, save for your children's future, and manage the day-to-day demands of living on a modest salary. But the wrong one? They can sell you products you don't need, put you in risky investments, or charge you fees that quietly bleed your finances over time. This chapter gives you a framework to approach that first meeting like a professional conversation, not a passive one.

Interviewing a financial advisor isn't just smart—it's necessary. You're hiring someone to help manage your money, your goals, and possibly even your legacy. Yet most teachers sit down with whoever their district partners with, or the rep who hands out donuts in the teacher's lounge, and never ask deeper questions. You wouldn't hire a contractor to remodel your home without reviewing their past work and asking about permits. So why treat your financial future with any less scrutiny? Here's your guide. Below are 25 questions you can ask in a financial advisor interview. Use them all. Take notes. Listen carefully. Your future deserves this level of attention.

1. Are you a fiduciary? (Will you always act in my best financial interest, legally and ethically?)
2. How do you get paid? (Fee-only, commission-based, salary, or a combination?)
3. What licenses, credentials, or certifications do you hold? (CFP®, CPA, Series 7, etc.)
4. Do you have experience working with public school teachers or government employees?
5. What services do you offer? (Investment advice, retirement planning, budgeting, insurance?)
6. How do you approach long-term planning for educators with pensions and 403(b)s?
7. Can you walk me through how you would build a plan for someone like me?
8. How often will we meet, and how will I be updated about my progress?
9. Do you receive compensation for recommending certain financial products?
10. Can I see a sample financial plan you've created for another (anonymous) educator?
11. Do you sell insurance products? If so, which ones, and how are you compensated?
12. What's your investment philosophy, and how do you choose funds or assets?
13. How do you handle market downturns or financial crises with your clients?
14. Will you help me evaluate my pension, service credit, and buyback options?
15. Can you help me decide when to retire, based on both finances and benefits?
16. Are you familiar with public student loan forgiveness (PSLF) and other teacher-specific programs?
17. How will you help me plan for rising healthcare costs in retirement?
18. Do you provide tax planning or coordinate with CPAs?

19. If you work in a team or firm, who else will be involved in my planning?
20. How accessible are you between meetings? Can I email or call with questions?
21. What's your process for helping clients through big life changes—divorce, job changes, death in the family?
22. Do you work with educators who also have side income or summer jobs?
23. What's your process for evaluating financial products you recommend?
24. How do you ensure your clients don't outlive their money?
25. What happens if I decide to stop working with you—are there fees or complications?

These aren't just questions—they're the foundation of your financial safety. They help you sniff out red flags, assess whether an advisor understands your unique situation, and establish boundaries from the start. It's okay to take your time, and it's okay to say no. Interview multiple advisors, compare their answers, and go with the one who respects your intelligence, aligns with your values, and empowers you to make better decisions.

You don't need to become a financial expert to advocate for yourself. You just need the right tools and the right questions. Think of this process the way you'd prepare a student for a research paper—you're not giving them answers, you're showing them how to ask better questions. That's what builds confidence. That's what builds knowledge. And that's what gives you the power to shape your financial future on your terms.

Chapter 29: Fee-Only, Fiduciary, or Commission-Based – Understanding Who's Really on Your Side

There are few decisions more important to your financial life than choosing the right advisor. Yet many teachers—stretched thin on time and patience—default to the representative who happens to show up in their staff lounge or leave a flyer in their mailbox. It feels convenient. Familiar. Sometimes even endorsed. But the person who hands you a brochure for a 403(b) plan may not be working in your best interest. This chapter is about learning who's really sitting on your side of the table. And to do that, you need to understand the differences between fee-only, fiduciary, and commission-based financial advisors.

Let's start with the term "fiduciary." This is not just a buzzword—it's a legal standard. A fiduciary is required by law to act in your best interest. That means they must put your needs ahead of their own profits. If a fiduciary advisor recommends a financial product or strategy, it has to be based on what's best for you—not what pays them the highest commission. That may seem like common sense, but not every advisor is held to that standard. Many aren't. Fiduciaries are usually fee-only, which means they charge a flat rate, an hourly fee, or a percentage of the assets they manage for you.

On the other hand, commission-based advisors are paid when they sell you a product—like an annuity, a mutual fund, or an insurance policy. This doesn't automatically make them unethical or ill-intentioned, but it creates a built-in conflict of interest. If someone makes more money by steering you into one product over another, can you trust that their recommendation is fully unbiased? It's a question worth asking. Many commission-based advisors work under what's called the "suitability" standard. That means their recommendation must be "suitable" for your situation, but not necessarily the best available option.

Then there are dually registered advisors—those who are both fiduciaries and commission-based, depending on what service they're offering. One moment, they're required to act in your best interest; the next, they might be allowed to sell you a commission-based product that's merely "suitable." That blurry line can be confusing for teachers who just want to trust the person helping them plan their retirement. If you're going to work with a dually registered advisor, be sure you understand when they're acting as a fiduciary and when they're not.

A fee-only advisor does not accept commissions or kickbacks. Their compensation comes directly from you. That's it. This model tends to minimize conflicts of interest because your advisor doesn't benefit from selling you a particular product. Their job is to give you advice, not to make a sale. Fee-only advisors can charge in several ways: flat-fee planning (a one-time or annual rate), hourly consultations, or a percentage of assets under management. While some teachers may balk at the cost, remember: you are paying for objective guidance. And in the long run, that clarity can save you far more than it costs.

Let's talk about the financial reps who walk into schools offering 403(b)s. Many are not fiduciaries. Many are tied to specific companies. Many are compensated when you choose the product they're selling. That's not necessarily predatory—but it does mean you should pause before signing anything. If you can't clearly understand how that person is being paid, that's a red flag. Ask them if they are a fiduciary. Ask if they receive commissions. Ask how they are licensed and what standard they're held to. A transparent advisor won't flinch at those questions.

A big problem in the education space is the lack of regulation around retirement plan vendors. Unlike corporate 401(k) plans, which are typically centralized and vetted, many school districts allow multiple 403(b) vendors with widely different fee structures and investment options. This creates a wild-west environment where high-fee annuities and opaque funds are too often the norm. A fiduciary or fee-only advisor can help you sort through those options and avoid long-term traps that eat away at your returns.

So what should you look for in an advisor? Look for someone who is a **Registered Investment Advisor (RIA)** or works at a firm registered with the SEC. Look for the **CFP® (Certified Financial Planner)** designation. Ask for a written fiduciary oath. Find someone who specializes in working with teachers or public servants. You don't need someone who knows how to help a billionaire shelter their wealth—you need someone who understands pensions, PSLF, classroom budgets, and the reality of having to work a second job in the summer.

A great advisor will educate you, not just execute transactions. They'll teach you how to think long-term. They'll help you avoid the trap of chasing hot tips in the teacher lounge or defaulting to whatever plan is easiest. And they won't push you into products you don't understand. If you feel confused, pressured, or rushed—that's your cue to pause. Financial planning should never feel like a sales pitch.

At the end of the day, your advisor should be someone who builds your confidence—not someone who creates more questions than answers. Whether you're starting your first Roth IRA or considering a pension buyback, you deserve advice that's rooted in your best interest. You don't have to become a financial expert overnight. But you do have to be willing to ask the hard questions, demand transparency, and remember: your paycheck may be limited, but your financial power is not. It just takes the right guide to help you activate it.

Part IV: The Pre-Retirement Chapter – Looking Ahead With Confidence

Part IV: The Pre-Retirement Chapter – Looking Ahead With Confidence is where the long game of a teaching career comes into full view. After decades of dedication, classroom moments, personal sacrifices, and evolving life responsibilities, this section speaks directly to educators in their 50s and 60s who are now shifting focus toward what comes next. But instead of anxiety or confusion, this part is built to bring clarity, peace of mind, and a plan.

These chapters walk readers through the often-overlooked details of preparing for retirement: how to understand your pension payout options, the tax implications of a lump sum versus an annuity, how 403(b)s and 457(b)s fit into the picture, and how to project what your monthly income will actually look like. We address Social Security timing, Medicare planning, legacy goals, and how to structure spending in the first ten years of retirement. Importantly, it's not just about numbers—it's about identity, purpose, and lifestyle.

We also dispel common myths and mistakes: that all pensions are the same, that teachers can't afford to retire early, or that you don't need estate planning if you "don't have much." For educators who are part of two-teacher households or single teachers supporting adult children or aging parents, we provide compassionate and tailored guidance. You'll also read about how to vet end-of-career financial professionals, what to do if you've never met with an advisor before, and how to avoid late-career financial missteps.

This section encourages teachers to retire with dignity and strategy—not just hoping it will work out, but knowing exactly how and why it will. Because when your career winds down, your financial confidence should rise. This part of the book is your roadmap for finishing strong and protecting what you've built.

Chapter 30: How to Know If You're on Track for Retirement

For many teachers, retirement feels more like a vague concept than a concrete financial milestone. Unlike professions with clear-cut 401(k) benchmarks or corporate matches, educators often rely on a blend of pension promises, optional savings plans, and Social Security benefits (if applicable). But knowing whether you're truly on track isn't just about what's on paper—it's about understanding how those pieces fit together to support the life you want post-classroom. This chapter is here to help you map that journey, regardless of whether retirement is 30 years away or just around the corner.

Start by identifying what "retirement" actually means to you. For some teachers, it's the age they can finally leave the profession with full pension benefits. For others, it's a phased exit into part-time tutoring or consulting. Define your version first. Once you've done that, work backward to assess your timeline, income goals, and likely expenses. Retirement planning isn't about a magic number—it's about cash flow. Will your pension and savings provide enough to cover your fixed costs, healthcare, travel, and emergencies? If not, you're not alone—but it does mean you'll need to take action now.

The first critical step is knowing your pension formula. Most public school teachers have access to a defined benefit pension plan, which calculates your monthly income based on years of service and final average salary. But the formulas vary widely by state and district. Some calculate based on your highest 3 years of salary; others use your last 5. Some require 20 years to vest; others allow you to retire after 30 years of service, regardless of age. Pull your pension estimate from your district's HR portal or call the plan administrator directly. Too many teachers retire without ever fully understanding what they're owed.

Next, take inventory of all supplemental retirement savings. Do you have a 403(b)? A Roth IRA? A 457(b) plan? How much is in each, and are you contributing regularly? These plans are what bridge the gap between your pension income and your retirement expenses. If you're not maximizing your contributions, consider increasing them gradually—even just $50 more per paycheck. Compound interest is on your side, especially if you're still more than 10 years out from retirement. If you're within five years, it's still not too late to ramp up your contributions aggressively.

Then, look at your retirement timeline and estimate your income replacement rate. Most financial planners recommend aiming for 70-80% of your pre-retirement income in retirement. For teachers, that often comes from a mix of pension (which might replace 40-60% of income), Social Security (if you're eligible), and personal savings. Run a retirement projection using free online calculators or meet with a professional who can model your scenario. The earlier you do this, the more options you have to adjust course.

It's also essential to factor in healthcare. If you retire before 65, you'll need a plan to cover insurance until Medicare kicks in. Some districts offer retiree medical benefits; others don't. Understand your specific situation. COBRA might be available for a limited time, or you might need to buy a policy on the individual marketplace. Healthcare can be one of your largest expenses in early retirement, so don't ignore it when running the numbers.

Another overlooked area: inflation. Today's expenses won't be tomorrow's expenses. Even with a strong pension, if your cost of living increases and your pension doesn't adjust adequately (some plans have limited cost-of-living adjustments), your purchasing power could erode over time. This is where having investment income—even modest—can help offset those changes and preserve your quality of life in retirement.

Now ask yourself: Are you mentally ready for retirement? Financial readiness and emotional readiness are deeply linked. If you're financially able to retire but haven't considered how you'll spend your days, where you'll find purpose, and how you'll handle transitions in identity, you may struggle. Talk to retired colleagues. Journal about what a "good retirement" looks like. Build a post-retirement routine before you walk away. The money matters, but so does the mindset.

Finally, revisit your plan annually. Life changes. Salaries change. Health changes. Family needs shift. Schedule a yearly "retirement check-in" where you review your pension estimates, savings growth, healthcare options, and projected expenses. Think of this like a parent-teacher conference—except the student is your future self. Stay engaged with the process, and don't be afraid to seek out a fiduciary advisor for a second opinion.

Being "on track" for retirement isn't about perfection. It's about preparedness. It's about asking the right questions now so that you don't wake up five years too late with regret. As a teacher, you've guided countless students to stay organized, think ahead, and manage their time. Now, it's your turn. Retirement is coming. You deserve to meet it with confidence—and with a plan that reflects everything you've worked so hard for.

Chapter 31: Understanding Your Pension Payout Options – Lump Sum vs. Monthly Income

For many teachers, the pension is more than a retirement benefit—it's a promise. After decades of early mornings, parent-teacher conferences, curriculum shifts, and deep emotional investment in your students, you deserve a financial foundation that honors that service. But the closer you get to retirement, the more you realize that the decisions you make about your pension aren't simple. One of the most important decisions you'll face is whether to take your pension as a lump sum or as a monthly income for life. This chapter is here to walk with you through that choice. We're not here to give you the "right answer," because there isn't one. We're here to help you ask the right questions.

Let's start with what each option actually means. Taking your pension as a lump sum means receiving a one-time payout of the present value of your pension. It becomes your responsibility to manage that money for the rest of your life. Opting for monthly income, on the other hand, means you receive a set payment every month for as long as you live, possibly with options for your spouse after your death. Both choices have merit. Both have risks. And both depend heavily on your personal life, goals, and risk tolerance.

There's an emotional aspect to this choice that doesn't get discussed enough. A lump sum might feel like freedom. Control. The ability to invest, spend, or leave a legacy on your own terms. But it can also feel overwhelming. What if you make a mistake? What if the markets dip? What if you live longer than expected and the money runs out? Meanwhile, monthly payments can feel like security. Like a steady rhythm that mimics your paycheck. But that rhythm can also feel restrictive. What if inflation eats away at your purchasing power? What if you need a large amount of money suddenly for a health issue or helping a family member?

Now, let's talk taxes. Lump sum distributions are often rolled over into an IRA to avoid immediate taxes, which gives you control over how and when the money is taxed. But if you cash it out directly, it could push you into a higher tax bracket and trigger penalties. Monthly income, on the other hand, is taxed as ordinary income each year. For some teachers, spreading the tax burden out over time is more manageable. Others prefer having more control and strategic flexibility with a rollover.

Let's also talk about longevity. If you have a family history of long life, monthly payments might look attractive. If you're in poor health, a lump sum might allow you to use or gift your money more freely. But the real question is, how do you want to structure your financial life in retirement? What will give you peace of mind? What will align with your values, responsibilities, and aspirations?

If you're married or have dependents, this decision has ripple effects. Joint survivor benefits might reduce your monthly income slightly, but offer financial continuity for your spouse. Lump sum payouts might give you more flexibility to help adult children, grandchildren, or causes you care about. But with flexibility comes responsibility. You become the pension manager, the investment strategist, the protector of the principal.

You also need to consider your relationship with money. Are you comfortable managing large sums? Do you have a trusted advisor or support system? Have you navigated major financial decisions in the past with confidence? Or do you feel more secure with a structured, predictable payment that you don't have to think about? Be honest with yourself about your money mindset. There's no shame in choosing the path that gives you the most peace.

The market matters too. If interest rates are low when your pension offers a lump sum, the payout might be higher than if rates are high. That's because lump sum values are calculated based on actuarial tables and interest rate assumptions. You may want to review the current rates and ask your HR or pension office to provide the calculations. Then, run projections for both paths with your financial advisor—or on your own using conservative estimates.

Finally, think about what you want retirement to *feel* like. Do you want predictability? Autopilot? Structure? Or do you want flexibility, investment growth potential, and autonomy? Both routes have trade-offs, and the best decision is the one that aligns with your reality, not someone else's opinion.

You don't have to decide overnight. And you certainly don't have to decide alone. But you do have to be honest with yourself about what you want your retirement to look like, and what kind of responsibility you're willing to carry. There are no guarantees—only trade-offs. The good news? As a teacher, you already know how to manage trade-offs. You do it every day in the classroom. Now it's time to do it for your future.

Chapter 32: Social Security for Teachers – WEP, GPO, and What It Means for You

Let's talk about something that gets ignored way too often: Social Security. Specifically, what Social Security looks like for teachers. You'd think it would be pretty straightforward—pay into the system, get your benefits. But in the teaching profession, things are rarely that simple. Depending on your state and district, you may have been contributing to Social Security, or you may have been part of a pension system that opted out. That decision—one you likely didn't even make yourself—can dramatically impact your retirement future. And if you're like most educators, you didn't find out about it until you were years into your career, or worse, just a few years from retirement.

That's where the Windfall Elimination Provision (WEP) and the Government Pension Offset (GPO) come into play. These aren't just acronyms. They are real policies that can reduce your Social Security benefits. For some teachers, the WEP lowers your personal benefit. For others, the GPO slashes your spousal or survivor benefits. In plain terms, you could be earning less from Social Security than you expected—sometimes significantly less—because you worked as a public servant. And no, it's not exactly fair.

You need to know whether you are affected. Not every teacher is. Some work in districts that pay into Social Security, others do not. And even within the same state, it can vary by district. Start by checking your Social Security statement and your pension documentation. If you see language about "non-covered employment," that's your red flag. You need to dig deeper.

Let's clarify the WEP first. The Windfall Elimination Provision reduces your own Social Security benefit if you also receive a pension from work where you didn't pay into Social Security. So if you spent 30 years teaching in a state without Social Security coverage and then took a part-time job at a bookstore for a few years where you did pay into the system, your Social Security benefit will be reduced. The logic, flawed as it is, is that your short contribution period creates an artificially inflated benefit under the regular calculation, so the WEP dials it back. There are formulas, thresholds, and exceptions—so yes, this is an area where talking to a financial professional can help.

Now, the GPO. The Government Pension Offset affects your ability to collect spousal or survivor Social Security benefits if you also receive a government pension from non-covered work. Basically, your teacher's pension could wipe out most or all of what you might

Chapter 33: Healthcare After Retirement – What You Must Plan For Now

When teachers think about retirement, the first thing that often comes to mind is the pension they've been building for decades. Maybe a 403(b) account comes next. But one of the most overlooked yet financially critical parts of retirement is healthcare. For many educators, the assumption is that retirement will bring peace, stability, and fewer expenses—but without a plan for healthcare, it can also bring massive, unexpected costs. Retiree health expenses can range from manageable to overwhelming, and understanding the landscape early is the key to staying ahead.

First, it's important to recognize that Medicare does not kick in until age 65. So, if you retire early—say at 58 or 60—you'll need to cover the gap years. Some school districts offer retiree health benefits that extend until Medicare eligibility, but these are becoming less common. If your district does offer this bridge coverage, know the terms and the cost. What percentage will you pay? Does your spouse qualify? What happens if your partner is younger and not yet Medicare-eligible? These are the questions to ask HR before you submit that retirement paperwork.

Even once Medicare begins, it's not free. Medicare Part B comes with a monthly premium, and if you choose supplemental coverage or Medicare Advantage, you'll need to budget for that as well. Many retired teachers are surprised to learn that Medicare doesn't cover long-term care, dental, vision, or hearing aids. You'll need to consider whether to buy additional insurance, build savings for out-of-pocket costs, or both. Start pricing those policies now, not when you're already retired.

Another crucial piece is understanding how your pension and Social Security (if applicable) affect your Medicare premiums. Higher-income retirees pay more for Medicare Part B and Part D under a rule called IRMAA (Income-Related Monthly Adjustment Amount). Your pension income could bump you into that bracket. That means planning isn't just about how much you'll spend, but also how your income is structured.

Long-term care is perhaps the elephant in the room. Whether you call it assisted living, memory care, or skilled nursing, the costs are real and rarely covered by traditional health insurance or Medicare. Teachers, like anyone else, are living longer, which is a gift—but also a financial liability if not planned for. You can explore long-term care insurance, hybrid life policies with LTC riders, or even Medicaid planning. Start those conversations while you're still working.

Consider the tax implications too. Withdrawals from your 403(b) or IRA to cover health costs are taxed as ordinary income. Health Savings Accounts (HSAs), on the other hand, can offer triple tax advantages—but you can't contribute to an HSA once you're on Medicare. That makes it smart to contribute aggressively to an HSA during your final working years if your district offers a high-deductible health plan.

One often-overlooked aspect is planning for a surviving spouse. If you pass away, will your spouse still be covered under any retiree plan? Will their income drop? Will they have access to affordable care? Teachers are often the primary source of stable benefits in a household. If that benefit ends with you, you need to prepare for what happens next.

The emotional side of this planning can't be ignored either. Many educators are so used to the school system handling their insurance logistics that transitioning to managing it independently in retirement feels overwhelming. You're not alone in feeling that way. That's why it's important to work with someone who understands not just insurance but the specific needs of public educators. Whether that's a fiduciary advisor, a retirement specialist, or a trusted colleague who has already retired—build your team now.

The sooner you begin mapping out your post-retirement healthcare plan, the more choices you'll have and the more control you'll feel. You're not planning for disaster—you're building a safety net. And that, more than anything, lets you enjoy your retirement with confidence and clarity.

Chapter 34: Creating a Withdrawal Strategy – 403(b), 457, IRA, and Pension Timing

When a teacher transitions from the daily rhythm of classroom life to the unfamiliar pace of retirement, one of the most important financial decisions they'll face is how to access the money they worked so hard to save. Retirement isn't just about stopping work; it's about starting a new phase of financial living. And while saving over the years is challenging, creating a withdrawal strategy is where many educators feel overwhelmed. The good news is that with the right approach, you can turn your pension, 403(b), 457 plan, and IRAs into reliable streams of income that support your lifestyle, protect your longevity, and minimize your tax burden.

Let's start with a simple but often misunderstood truth: not all retirement accounts should be touched at the same time or in the same way. Your pension may offer monthly income that begins automatically at retirement, but your 403(b) and 457 plans are more flexible, and that flexibility can either be a gift or a trap. If you begin withdrawing from these accounts too soon, you may pay penalties or deplete them faster than necessary. If you wait too long, you may be forced into larger required minimum distributions (RMDs) that bump you into a higher tax bracket. Understanding sequencing is the key.

One of the smartest moves a retiring teacher can make is to review their pension payout options first. Does it make more sense to choose a single life annuity, a joint survivor option, or a lump sum rollover? Each choice has different implications for income reliability, taxes, and spousal protection. This decision sets the tone for the rest of your withdrawal strategy. For example, if you opt for a smaller monthly pension to protect your spouse, you might need to draw more aggressively from your 403(b) in the early years.

Next, consider how your 403(b) and 457 plans interact. Unlike 403(b)s, which have a 10% penalty for early withdrawal before age 59½, 457 plans often allow penalty-free access at separation from service. This gives teachers a strategic tool: using the 457 for early retirement years, then switching to the 403(b) or IRA later. Think of it as a financial bridge to get you to age 59½ or Social Security eligibility without dipping into taxable brokerage accounts.

Tax efficiency is another critical factor. If you have a mix of pre-tax (traditional 403(b), 457, or IRA) and post-tax (Roth IRA or Roth 403(b)) funds, you can control your taxable income by choosing where to withdraw from each year. One popular approach is to draw from taxable or Roth assets early in retirement to allow tax-deferred accounts to continue growing—or to strategically convert some of those funds to Roth during low-tax years. Doing so can significantly reduce your lifetime tax liability.

You also need to think about required minimum distributions (RMDs), which start at age 73. If you have large balances in your 403(b), 457, or traditional IRA, you could be forced to take more income than you need, leading to higher taxes and potential Medicare premium increases. Planning ahead—perhaps by doing Roth conversions in your 60s or withdrawing slightly more than needed in your early retirement years—can give you more control down the road.

Social Security adds another layer of complexity. Many teachers are impacted by the Windfall Elimination Provision (WEP) and Government Pension Offset (GPO), which can reduce or eliminate Social Security benefits if you have a pension from work where you didn't pay into Social Security. Timing when and how you claim Social Security—if you're eligible—should factor into your overall withdrawal plan. It may be wise to delay Social

Security to maximize benefits, especially if your pension is lower than expected.

Don't forget the role of inflation and longevity. A withdrawal plan isn't static. What works at 62 might not be sustainable at 82. Inflation can erode your purchasing power, especially if your pension isn't cost-of-living adjusted. That means your 403(b) or IRA may need to cover more of your basic expenses later in life. A smart withdrawal strategy anticipates this by tapering spending in some areas, adjusting asset allocation, or building in guaranteed income sources.

Finally, keep in mind that your withdrawal strategy should be a living plan, not a one-time decision. Life happens. Markets fluctuate. Needs change. You may face unexpected healthcare expenses, need to help a family member financially, or want to travel more in certain years. Having flexibility built into your plan—and revisiting it annually with a financial advisor who understands educator benefits—can make all the difference.

In the end, your withdrawal strategy is about much more than math. It's about aligning your money with your life's rhythm, honoring the decades you spent educating others, and giving yourself the confidence to enjoy the retirement you've earned. Whether you're starting from scratch or fine-tuning a nearly finalized plan, the goal is not perfection—it's clarity, control, and peace of mind.

Chapter 35: What Happens If You Switch Districts or Leave Education?

Switching school districts or leaving education entirely is one of the most significant financial decisions a teacher can make—one that ripples across retirement accounts, pension eligibility, health insurance, and even your sense of identity. The teaching profession is unlike most other careers in that so many of your long-term benefits are tied to staying in one place for a long time. So when you consider walking away, even if it's for a great reason—a better school culture, a higher-paying opportunity, or a completely different career path—it's important to know exactly what's on the table, and what's at stake.

Let's begin with the pension system, since for many teachers, it's the foundation of their retirement plan. Pensions are governed by state rules, and each state has different vesting requirements. If you leave before you're vested—often after five or ten years—you may not receive any pension income, or only a return of your contributions without interest. This could mean walking away from tens of thousands of dollars in retirement income. On the other hand, staying just a few more years could unlock significant future benefits. That's why understanding your exact pension vesting timeline is crucial before making a move.

Then there's the question of portability. Unlike a 401(k), most teacher pension systems don't travel with you across state lines. If you move from a district in New York to one in Texas, you're starting a new pension timeline from scratch unless the two systems have reciprocity agreements—and most don't. You may end up with two partial pensions that don't add up to a full one. Some teachers think they'll be able to "buy back" service years later, but that process is often complicated, expensive, and riddled with red tape. So before you take a new job, especially in another state, make sure you understand what you're keeping and what you're giving up.

Leaving education altogether comes with its own set of calculations. If you transition to a private-sector job, you'll likely move from a pension-based retirement system to one that relies on a 401(k) or individual retirement accounts (IRAs). While these accounts offer more portability and control, they also require you to be more proactive. You'll need to make investment decisions, track contributions, and think about how to replace the guaranteed income a pension would have provided. There's no right or wrong answer here—but there is a big difference between choosing a new path out of clarity versus leaping without a plan.

Healthcare is another critical factor. Many school districts offer subsidized healthcare for retired teachers who meet certain years-of-service requirements. If you leave early, you may forfeit access to these benefits, leaving you to navigate the private healthcare marketplace or rely on a spouse's plan. For some educators, this cost is manageable. For others, especially those with ongoing health issues or dependents to cover, it can be a dealbreaker. Before you make a change, calculate what your healthcare expenses would be and how they'll shift across time, especially in early retirement years before Medicare eligibility kicks in.

There's also the emotional layer. Teaching is more than a job—it's a calling, a community, and a big piece of how many educators see themselves. Leaving the profession, whether temporarily or permanently, can come with a sense of guilt, grief, or identity loss. It's important to acknowledge these emotions as part of your decision-making process. You're not just moving jobs—you're potentially redefining your sense of purpose. And that's not a decision to rush.

If you're married to or living with another educator, the decision to leave education can also impact household finances in ways you may not expect. For example, two-teacher households often structure their finances around dual pension income and shared benefits. If one person leaves, it changes the equation. It may be wise to run the numbers on what life would look like with only one pension stream, especially if you're banking on that income to support children, debt payoff, or retirement travel goals. Financial planners who specialize in public employees can help with this modeling.

One action step you can take right now, even if you're only vaguely considering a change, is to request a copy of your pension benefit statement and service credit record. You can also ask HR to explain what would happen to your health insurance, accrued sick leave, and retirement accounts if you left. Get it in writing. These are the tools that allow you to make an informed decision, rather than one based on guesses or assumptions. Consider reviewing these documents with a financial advisor who understands public sector retirement systems.

There's also the strategic middle ground of leaving the classroom but not the profession. Roles in administration, curriculum development, educational nonprofits, or corporate training departments may allow you to use your teaching skills in new ways—without entirely severing ties with education. Some of these roles may even let you continue accruing pension service years, depending on how they're classified. It's worth exploring creative career pivots before assuming that leaving teaching means starting over from scratch.

This chapter doesn't exist to tell you whether to stay or go—it's here to make sure that if you do go, you're walking into your next chapter with open eyes, accurate numbers, and a plan. Your work matters, whether it's in a classroom or beyond it. So does your financial future. And both deserve the kind of respect that comes from informed, intentional decision-making—not reactive moves made in a moment of frustration or burnout. Take your time. Gather your data. And don't let anyone rush you through a choice that can reshape your life and legacy.

Chapter 36: Should You Retire Early or Stick It Out? Emotional and Financial Tradeoffs

There comes a point in every teacher's journey where the clock, the calendar, and the internal dialogue start to converge. You ask yourself quietly at first, then more frequently, "Could I retire early? Should I?" It's not just a financial question; it's an emotional crossroads. The classroom has been your rhythm for decades. The sounds of morning bells, the weight of lesson plans, the camaraderie in the teacher's lounge, the controlled chaos of the last day before summer—these moments aren't easily left behind. But neither is the mounting pressure. If you're reading this chapter, you're probably not here for abstract theory. You want to understand the tradeoffs of leaving early versus staying the course, and you want someone to break it down without sugarcoating or scolding.

Let's first acknowledge the very real fatigue. Teaching is not a job you coast through. It's physically demanding, emotionally exhausting, and often financially frustrating. Many educators in their 50s start dreaming about freedom—about waking up without a bell schedule or staff meeting. But what you dream about and what your retirement accounts can support may not always align. The first step in evaluating early retirement is getting brutally honest about your numbers. How much have you saved in your 403(b), 457 plan, IRA, or pension system? What will those distributions look like if you leave at 58 instead of 62? What would your monthly income actually be after taxes and healthcare costs? Run the numbers. And if you don't know how—get help. That knowledge alone might shift your timeline or give you a green light.

Now let's talk about healthcare, because this can be the cliff no one warns you about. If you leave your district before Medicare eligibility (typically age 65), how will you bridge the gap? Will your district offer retiree healthcare? If not, can you afford an ACA plan? What if your spouse is still working—can you get coverage through them? Early retirement without a healthcare strategy is like driving cross-country with no gas stations on the map. It's a risk that can burn through your savings faster than you expected. Healthcare isn't just about insurance—it's about preserving your quality of life. Don't skip this conversation.

But money isn't the only variable in this equation. For many teachers, identity is wrapped tightly around their role. You may be retiring from the job, but not from your sense of purpose. What will replace the emotional rewards of teaching? Have you thought about consulting, mentoring, substitute teaching a few days a week, or even tutoring online? Financially, these side gigs can stretch your savings further. Emotionally, they can provide structure and meaning. Retirement shouldn't feel like a void—it should feel like a transition into something that still reflects your values and talents, even if it's more flexible.

Another factor: social connections. School isn't just where you work; it's where you laugh, cry, vent, and connect with other adults who get it. Retiring early might improve your blood pressure, but it may also impact your social life more than you expect. Have you built a community outside of school? Are there organizations, clubs, or causes you've always wanted to join but never had time for? Just as you prepare financially, you need to prepare socially. Boredom and isolation are real risks that can dull the joy of financial freedom. Plan your days as much as you plan your dollars.

One important emotional tradeoff that doesn't get discussed enough is the guilt some teachers feel about leaving "early." You've spent your life helping others, and you might worry that retiring before full eligibility is somehow selfish or irresponsible. Let's be clear: it's not. You've already given more than most professions could ever ask for. If you've reached a place—emotionally, financially, and physically—where retirement feels like the right next chapter, you've earned it. But if you're still called to stay, even part-time, that's equally valid. Your worth isn't measured by years served—it's measured by the impact you've had.

Let's also address the pension penalty. Some states and districts impose sharp reductions in benefits for early retirement. You might lose out on cost-of-living adjustments or have your final average salary calculation reduced. Understand your specific pension formula. Call HR. Request projections. Know the difference between retiring at 55 vs. 60 vs. 65—not just the benefit difference, but the long-term effect on your total payout. Compound that over two or three decades, and it might shift your decision.

For some, the idea of working a few extra years just for the full pension feels like a trap. But for others, it's a safety net worth holding on to. Ask yourself: is staying longer just about the money, or do you still find joy in the work? Are you avoiding something else? Or chasing something that doesn't require full retirement to pursue? Get real with your motives. No one else can answer that for you.

Finally, consider the emotional legacy of your retirement decision. How do you want to feel looking back on this choice five years from now? Will you wish you left earlier to travel, to spend time with family, to pursue creative projects—or will you be glad you stayed, built a bigger pension, and walked away on your own terms? Only you can define your legacy, and that includes how and when you close the teaching chapter of your life.

There is no universally right answer to whether you should retire early or stick it out. There's only your answer—and it's one that should be built with clarity, not fear. The goal is to retire "to" something, not "from" something. Let that mindset shape your next move.

Chapter 37: Avoiding Retirement Jealousy – Everyone's Path Looks Different

You spend decades side by side in the teacher's lounge, attending in-service trainings, chaperoning prom, and surviving curriculum changes together. Then suddenly, a colleague announces they're retiring—early. They're off to a lake house in Michigan or starting a consulting business or taking a year to travel the world. You smile, congratulate them, even sign the card with a heartfelt message. But inside, something stings. You're not ready. Financially, emotionally, or logistically, retirement isn't on your immediate horizon. And it can feel like you're falling behind.

This feeling is more common than you think. Retirement jealousy is real, especially in education where comparison is baked into the culture—from classroom sizes and state test scores to who gets first pick of parking spots. When a peer retires early, it can trigger a wave of insecurity: Did they plan better? Do they know something I don't? Am I doing this wrong? These questions can quietly eat away at your confidence and sense of control.

But here's the truth: every retirement path is different because every teaching journey is different. Maybe your colleague worked in a district with stronger pension contributions. Maybe they had a spouse with health benefits that freed them to retire sooner. Maybe they inherited a house, avoided student loans, or simply had different priorities. It doesn't make them smarter, more disciplined, or more worthy of rest. It just means their path was theirs. Yours is yours.

Rather than viewing their retirement as a reflection of your shortcomings, use it as a moment of reflection. What does financial peace look like for you? Do you want to work part-time after you retire, or never work again? Would you rather have a paid-off house or a small mortgage and more liquid savings? Your answers matter—and they will shape your plan far more than someone else's timeline ever could.

It's also important to recognize that early retirement is not always the happy ending it appears to be. Some early retirees feel isolated, miss the structure of teaching, or wrestle with unexpected financial stress. What looks perfect on the surface may be more complicated in practice. That's why your plan needs to be built on clarity, not comparison.

If you're feeling envious or disoriented when someone else retires, that's a signal to check in with your numbers and your goals. Have you met with a retirement planner to assess your pension payout options? Do you know how Social Security will or won't fit into your future income? Have you calculated your monthly expenses in retirement versus your expected income streams? Ground yourself in your own facts.

It might help to journal out what you really want from retirement. Is it rest? Freedom? Time with grandkids? The ability to volunteer, create, or explore? Then look at what pieces you can start building now—even if retirement is still 5, 10, or 15 years away. Progress is not always about leaving the profession. Sometimes, it's about staying with greater peace.

Also, consider having honest conversations with those who retire ahead of you. Ask them what they wish they'd known. You might find they envy something about your situation, too—whether it's your current flexibility, your proximity to full vesting, or even your daily connection to students. Retirement isn't a finish line; it's just a different lane.

Ultimately, there is no single map for retiring well. There are only the routes that match your life, your family, and your finances. The key is not racing to someone else's destination, but walking confidently in your own direction—knowing that fulfillment, purpose, and financial wellness are not one-size-fits-all outcomes.

If you ever feel like you're behind, remember that financial well-being is not just about age or assets. It's about alignment. Is your life aligned with your values? Are your money choices giving you peace or pressure? Use those questions, not someone else's send-off party, to guide your next step.

Chapter 38: How to Create a Written Retirement Plan Without Feeling Overwhelmed

Retirement planning can feel like standing at the base of a mountain with no clear trail. For teachers who have spent decades pouring time, energy, and heart into others, the idea of mapping out the next 30 years of your own life can be both empowering and paralyzing. But the truth is, the most important part of any retirement plan is just starting it. Not perfecting it. Not understanding every tax code or investment strategy. Just getting it down on paper and building a framework that reflects your values, your goals, and the life you've earned.

The first step is giving yourself permission to plan for *you*. Teachers often spend their careers thinking about everyone else—the students, the parents, the school district. You're used to managing lesson plans, adapting to curveballs, and making magic with limited resources. Retirement planning asks you to take that same organizational mindset and turn it inward. It's not selfish. It's not extravagant. It's survival with intention. You've taught others to prepare for their future—now it's your turn.

Start by answering three grounding questions: What does retirement mean to you? What do you want your daily life to look like when you're no longer teaching full-time? And what are the non-negotiables—healthcare, housing, family support—that need to be funded? You don't need a spreadsheet or financial software to begin. You need clarity. That clarity becomes the lens through which every other decision is filtered. It also keeps you from falling into the comparison trap with colleagues who may retire earlier, later, or with different resources.

Your written plan should include a timeline. Not just when you want to retire, but when major financial events will occur. When will your pension kick in? When should you start drawing from your 403(b), 457, or IRA? When do you want your mortgage paid off? When will you qualify for Medicare? A simple chronological structure—year by year or in five-year blocks—gives shape to what otherwise feels like a giant fog of "someday."

Another key part of your written plan should be income sources. List them out: your pension, any supplemental retirement accounts, Social Security, annuities, rental income, part-time work, or spousal benefits. Seeing these written down creates a sense of security and direction. If you're not sure how much income to expect from each source, that's okay. Write what you know, highlight what you need to find out, and note who can help you (HR, a financial advisor, your spouse, etc.).

Don't forget to include a section about expenses—specifically, your projected monthly and annual retirement budget. You don't need it to be perfect. You just need a starting point. Will your home be paid off? Will you be traveling more or less than now? What will healthcare cost? What lifestyle changes do you anticipate? This part is less about restriction and more about awareness. When you know what you need, you can align your assets accordingly and reduce stress in the process.

Now, think about contingencies. What happens if you or your spouse experiences a major health issue? What if one of your adult children needs help? What if inflation outpaces your pension's cost-of-living adjustments? A good retirement plan doesn't just list the ideal—it acknowledges the unpredictable. You don't need to solve every what-if, but you should name them and list how you'd respond. That's the difference between reaction and readiness.

Finally, keep your written plan accessible and updated. This isn't a one-and-done document. It's a living roadmap. Set a date each year to review and revise it—maybe every summer after school lets out or during winter break. Add notes, questions, updates, and milestones. You might even keep a retirement journal alongside it—where you can reflect on what you're learning and how you feel about the transition ahead.

What makes this process less overwhelming is remembering that you don't have to do it all at once. A plan can start with one page, one question, one moment of reflection. Then it grows. Just like your career. The more time you give it, the clearer it becomes. And when the day comes to close your classroom door for the last time, you won't be stepping into the unknown—you'll be walking a path you already wrote, with wisdom, love, and purpose guiding the way.

Chapter 39: Leaving a Legacy – Teaching Your Family How to Manage Wealth (Big or Small)

Legacy means more than just leaving behind a sum of money; it means passing down values, habits, and tools that can help the next generation thrive, no matter the size of your estate. For teachers, who have spent a career shaping young minds and nurturing growth, there is something profoundly fitting about extending that mentorship to their own families through financial education. But most teachers don't get formal training on how to talk about money with their children or how to prepare their family for managing finances after they're gone. This chapter is about making that process approachable, meaningful, and aligned with the life you've built through education and service.

Start by recognizing that wealth is relative. You don't have to be a millionaire to leave a meaningful legacy. Maybe it's a paid-off home. Maybe it's a small pension. Maybe it's a modest but consistent investment account or simply the absence of debt. These are all assets. And they carry power when paired with clarity. One of the most helpful things you can do for your family is to document your assets, accounts, and final wishes in a way that is clear and accessible. Consider creating a "family financial binder" with login info, insurance policies, account statements, and a written letter explaining your intentions. Don't rely on memory or informal conversations. Give them a guide.

Many teachers underestimate the impact their financial behavior has on their children. You're teaching them about money whether you mean to or not. They see how you talk about bills, how you spend, how you give, and how you respond to financial stress. Part of legacy building is being intentional with those moments. If your children are young, involve them in budgeting decisions or let them help plan for back-to-school purchases. If they're older, share how your pension works, what your mortgage costs, and why you chose your retirement savings strategy. Normalize these conversations.

A written retirement plan, complete with beneficiary designations, powers of attorney, wills, and trusts (if applicable), is not just for the wealthy. Teachers who want to protect their families should consider working with a financial advisor or estate attorney to set these up properly. This is especially important if you have dependents, own property, or have remarried. Don't leave your loved ones guessing. Provide a structure.

One of the emotional barriers to legacy planning is the belief that there isn't "enough" to worry about. This mindset is common, but it can be harmful. If you've worked 25 or 30 years in education and built a pension, that's likely one of your family's most valuable lifetime assets. If you've raised responsible children, contributed to 403(b)s, or paid off a home, you've already laid the groundwork for multigenerational stability. It's not about the dollar amount. It's about making sure whatever you do have is understood, protected, and properly passed on.

Culturally, money conversations can feel taboo or uncomfortable. For many teachers, especially those from historically marginalized communities, money may have been a source of stress or secrecy growing up. Breaking that cycle can feel scary but empowering. Start by holding a family meeting. Frame it as a way to honor your values and teach financial confidence, not to scare anyone. You might begin by sharing your own journey—what you learned late, what you wish you'd known, and how you want to empower your family going forward.

Don't forget that legacy also includes generosity. If you're passionate about education, community service, or faith-based giving, consider documenting how you'd like to support those causes, either during your life or through your estate. That might mean setting up a scholarship fund, donating classroom supplies, or directing a portion of your retirement account to a nonprofit. Teaching your family about giving—how, when, and why—is just as important as teaching them to save.

Practical tools matter too. Consider encouraging your adult children or beneficiaries to work with a financial planner after your passing—especially if they are receiving life insurance, retirement distributions, or real estate assets. Without guidance, even a modest inheritance can be quickly lost to poor decisions. Part of your legacy might be modeling the wisdom of asking for help. Normalize financial advice as a strength, not a weakness.

Finally, consider writing a legacy letter. This is not a legal document, but a personal one. In it, you share your life values, hopes for your family, and the lessons you've learned—financial or otherwise. For teachers, this can be especially powerful. It's one last opportunity to educate, affirm, and leave a permanent reminder of who you were beyond the numbers. Whether you leave behind $10,000 or $1 million, that letter can be one of the most meaningful things your family receives.

Not every family will handle your legacy the way you want them to. But by preparing thoughtfully, documenting clearly, and communicating consistently, you increase the chances that your wealth—and your wisdom—will live on with dignity. There is no perfect plan, just progress. And every step you take toward clarity is a step toward peace of mind for everyone you love.

Part V: Financial Literacy and Leadership – Beyond the Classroom

Part V: Financial Literacy and Leadership – Beyond the Classroom explores what happens when educators apply their financial knowledge outside their own personal budgets and begin leading conversations in their schools, communities, and families. This section recognizes that teachers are not only role models in academics but also powerful agents of financial change. Whether it's helping a colleague understand their pension options, guiding a student who's curious about credit, or mentoring a new teacher who's overwhelmed by loan repayment, educators who gain financial clarity are uniquely positioned to lift others up.

This part dives into topics like how to start financial literacy clubs at school, how to become an advocate for better district-sponsored benefits, and how to influence policy by understanding where education funding really goes. It helps teachers build confidence in their voice—whether they're speaking at a union meeting, running for school board, or simply leading their own household with a clear financial strategy. It covers how to use your story to help others without overextending yourself, and how to protect your energy while still making an impact.

More than anything, Part V is about legacy—not just the money you leave behind, but the mindset, example, and education you pass forward. You don't need a financial planning degree to lead. You just need to care, stay curious, and share what you've learned. This section will show you how.

Chapter 40: Starting a Financial Literacy Book Club With Fellow Teachers

Starting a financial literacy book club with your fellow teachers might sound like one more thing on an already full plate, but in practice, it can be one of the most empowering, community-building steps you take. Think about it: educators spend their days pouring into others, and yet often lack the time, resources, or support to invest in their own financial well-being. A book club is more than a shared reading list. It becomes a space for reflection, solidarity, and strategy—a chance to learn not just from the pages in front of you, but from the lived experiences of the teachers sitting beside you. If you're feeling uncertain about your money or isolated in your financial questions, you're not alone. And this kind of collective learning is proof of that.

You don't need to be a financial expert to start. You need curiosity, consistency, and a bit of coordination. The most successful book clubs often begin with a small, intentional group—maybe four to six teachers from your grade level team, department, or school friends you already trust. Set a regular time and place that feels low-pressure: an hour after school once a month in someone's classroom, a Saturday morning coffee shop meetup, or even a virtual session after bedtime routines. The key is to make it doable. Teachers are tired. If the vibe is just one more obligation, it won't stick. If the tone is supportive and encouraging, it becomes something people actually look forward to.

Choosing your first book matters, but not in the way people often think.

Don't overanalyze whether the book covers everything perfectly. The goal isn't to become certified financial planners; the goal is to start talking. Pick a book that feels accessible, engaging, and relevant to the questions you and your colleagues are already wrestling with. It could be about budgeting, debt freedom, investing basics, or mindset. Ideally, it includes examples that speak to the realities of public service, middle-class income, or education careers. You could even start with this very book. Whatever you choose, begin with chapters that spark conversation, not just quiet reading.

Structure matters—but it doesn't have to be rigid. Consider opening each meeting with a simple prompt: What's one insight or question you had from this chapter? What's one thing you tried or want to try? What confused or challenged you? Keep it open and judgment-free. The point is not to compete over who's "doing it right" financially, but to create space where people can process together. Over time, these sessions can include guest speakers (local credit union reps, 403(b) vendors, estate attorneys), themed nights (budgeting bootcamp, tax Q&A), or workshops where teachers bring in their pay stubs and do a side-by-side breakdown together.

You'll be surprised by how quickly the ripple effect spreads. A teacher shares how they finally started a Roth IRA after the group discussion. Another one got clarity on their student loan forgiveness options and told their friend across the hall. One week you're chatting about compound interest; the next week, someone brings their spouse or sibling to join in. Momentum builds when shame lifts—and there is something profoundly powerful about naming financial fears in a room of peers who get it. It turns isolation into action.

You may hit snags. Someone might dominate the conversation. Another member might ghost the group after a couple meetings. A discussion might veer into territory that feels uncomfortable, political, or deeply personal. That's okay. You're not trying to run a flawless seminar. You're trying to build trust. When things feel off, name it gently. Revisit your group's purpose. Set shared norms early on—confidentiality, respect, no "shoulding" others, space for questions—and return to those as needed. Flexibility and clarity are your tools.

Eventually, this book club can become more than a meeting. It can evolve into a movement inside your school. Imagine it branching into student workshops, family financial nights, or PD sessions during in-service days. Imagine it informing your next union negotiation conversation. Imagine it equipping your mentees as they begin their careers. You might even find yourself writing your own curriculum or leading district-wide sessions because of what started as a Thursday-night potluck and paperback.

And yes, this can help you too—personally, financially, emotionally. Being surrounded by colleagues who are doing the same work, earning the same salary, and facing the same stressors makes for one of the most uniquely relevant financial learning environments possible. There's power in that specificity. You don't need to explain why the $500 classroom stipend matters so much, or why summers off aren't really "off" at all. Everyone already knows. That shared context makes the advice feel less abstract and more actionable.

If you've been waiting for the right moment, this is it. If you've been hoping someone else would get it started, maybe that someone is you. The courage to launch a book club isn't about being the expert. It's about caring enough to gather people, ask honest questions, and learn out loud. You won't just become more financially literate—you'll become more connected, more empowered, and more prepared to model the kind of leadership that extends beyond the classroom.

And when the school year ends, and your club members reflect on what they gained, chances are they won't just remember the charts or the chapters. They'll remember the conversations, the laughter, the support, and the feeling of finally talking about money in a way that felt safe, hopeful, and deeply human. That's where real literacy begins.

Chapter 41: How to Have Age-Appropriate Money Talks With Your Kids

Talking to your kids about money doesn't have to be awkward or complicated. In fact, the earlier you begin, the more natural it becomes. The key is meeting them at their developmental stage with honesty and simplicity. As a teacher, you already know how to explain complex topics in age-appropriate ways—you do it all day. The same skills you use in your classroom apply at home. Whether your child is four or fourteen, there are meaningful and empowering ways to open the conversation about finances.

When children are young, they learn best through observation and repetition. At this age, money talks aren't about stocks or student loans—they're about identifying coins, counting dollars, and understanding the basics of exchange. Let them hand the cashier the money at the grocery store. Show them how change works. Explain that money is earned through work and that it's something we have to manage carefully. These lessons set a foundation that will grow with them.

Elementary school is a perfect time to introduce concepts like saving, spending, and sharing. Consider giving your child a small allowance and dividing it into jars or envelopes: one for saving, one for spending, and one for giving. Let them experience the pride of saving for something they want, the responsibility of deciding what to buy, and the joy of helping someone else. These are lessons that stick—and they don't require lectures or fear-based messaging.

Middle schoolers are ready for more complex ideas. This is the age when peer pressure begins to show up in spending habits, and it's essential to help them develop a sense of financial self-worth. Talk openly about your own budget. Let them see you making choices based on your values, not just wants. Teach them about delayed gratification, comparison shopping, and the difference between needs and wants. You might even help them open a savings account to begin learning how banking works.

By high school, your child should be introduced to real-world money management. Discuss how credit works, how student loans function, and what it means to live within your means. Help them build a simple budget for their part-time job or allowance. Talk about the cost of college and walk them through your FAFSA conversations. Let them sit in on a financial planning meeting if you're comfortable. The goal is to normalize these discussions, not keep them hidden until adulthood.

Throughout all stages, resist the urge to make money a taboo or stressful topic. Kids pick up on emotional cues quickly. If money always seems to bring tension in the household, they'll internalize that. Instead, aim to speak about money in calm, matter-of-fact ways. It's okay to admit that something is expensive or that you're choosing not to spend on something right now. These moments aren't failures—they're lessons in boundaries and intentionality.

As a teacher, you may feel the strain of modeling financial literacy when your own budget feels tight. But your transparency and care can be incredibly powerful. It's okay to say, "We're choosing to save for a family goal," or "We want to spend wisely so we can enjoy things later." Your kids don't need you to be wealthy—they need you to be wise. Your lived example matters more than a perfectly balanced financial portfolio.

One of the most important steps you can take is to continue learning together. Read age-appropriate books on money. Watch short videos or documentaries. Reflect on commercials and advertisements together—what are they trying to make you feel? Why do we want what we want? These conversations help kids think critically and develop healthy skepticism in a consumer culture.

As your children grow into young adults, continue to be a safe place for financial discussions. Help them open their first checking account, choose their first credit card, and understand their first paycheck. Be willing to talk about your own money mistakes and what you've learned. There's no such thing as a perfect financial upbringing, but there is such a thing as a financially curious and confident child.

Some chapters don't need a tidy conclusion—just a clear beginning. This is one of those chapters. The most important thing is to start. Start small, start simply, but start. Your children are watching and learning. You don't have to be an expert—you just have to be engaged.

Chapter 42: Talking About Money With Students (When It's Age-Appropriate and Allowed)

It's a quiet moment between class transitions, and a student lingers at your desk. They ask you why taxes exist or what a credit score means. You pause, torn between wanting to teach something important and worrying about overstepping. As teachers, we're always balancing curriculum demands with real-world questions, and money is one of the most real-world topics there is. This chapter is about helping you navigate those moments with care, clarity, and confidence—especially when your school, district, or state has rules around what can and can't be taught about personal finance.

For many students, school is the only structured environment where they can safely learn about money. Yet very few receive any formal financial education before they graduate. That means the questions they ask you in the hallway, during advisory, or even in casual conversation might be some of their earliest exposures to financial thinking. As a teacher, you're not expected to be a certified financial planner. But you can be a guide. You can open doors of curiosity and point students toward reputable resources. You can model financial thinking that is grounded, nonjudgmental, and age-appropriate.

What you say, and how you say it, matters deeply. Talking to elementary students about needs vs. wants looks very different than explaining compounding interest to high schoolers. And talking about wealth inequality or generational debt carries emotional weight. That's why it's essential to adjust the scope, tone, and content of your conversations based on the age, maturity level, and background of your students. What's appropriate in one classroom may not land the same way in another. Sensitivity to culture, language, and lived experience must come first.

Let's also acknowledge the boundaries. You might want to talk about budgeting, credit cards, taxes, or even your own experiences with money—but depending on your district, you may need parental approval, administrative oversight, or alignment with state standards to do so. That doesn't mean you can't talk about money at all. It just means you need to understand the framework in which you're operating. Know your policy. If in doubt, collaborate with your administration or your school counselor. Financial literacy is too important to wing it, and too powerful to ignore.

There are creative ways to integrate money conversations without needing a full-on personal finance course. For example, use literature class to discuss characters' economic choices. Bring in math lessons about decimals or percentages by using sales tax or budgeting scenarios. Use social studies to examine how financial systems affect historical events. These small but intentional connections give students a foundation without crossing any policy lines.

Another entry point? Student-led inquiry. When students ask the questions, they invite you into a conversation rather than the other way around. That's a powerful shift. You're not giving a lesson; you're responding to curiosity. When done well, this approach builds trust, critical thinking, and real-world application. Keep your answers clear, neutral, and curiosity-driven. Instead of telling them what to do, ask them what they think—then gently guide the discussion toward facts, examples, and balanced insights.

Some teachers start after-school clubs, bring in guest speakers, or use resources like Junior Achievement, Next Gen Personal Finance, or local credit unions to supplement classroom learning. Others build classroom economies or mock investment projects, showing how saving, earning, spending, and giving all interact. If you choose to build something extracurricular, make sure you get proper permission and promote it inclusively so all students feel welcome.

Finally, understand that your role is less about having all the answers and more about being a consistent source of encouragement. Many students come from households where money is a source of stress, secrecy, or shame. Your openness can show them that financial questions are not only normal—they are necessary. You don't have to tell them what car to buy or how to use a credit card. You just have to be the kind of adult who listens, validates, and points them in the direction of learning.

This chapter doesn't end with a checklist or a punchline. It ends with a reflection: What's one conversation about money you wish someone had with you when you were younger? What would it have changed for you? Let that memory shape how you approach the next curious student who asks about money—because what you say next might stay with them for life.

Chapter 43: Teaching Students to Save, Budget, and Avoid Debt – A Personal Mission

Every teacher I know has a secret wish list of lessons they hope their students will remember long after the last test. For some, it's grammar rules or the scientific method. For others, it's the value of critical thinking or the power of empathy. But more and more educators are adding financial literacy to that wish list—especially the basics: saving, budgeting, and staying out of debt. These aren't just life skills. They're survival skills. And in communities where financial knowledge is scarce or withheld, they can be the keys that unlock entire futures. For many of us in the classroom, this mission to teach money is personal. We know what it feels like to learn the hard way, and we want better for the next generation.

If you've ever overheard students swapping stories about cash app transfers, sneaker resales, or how they plan to spend their next paycheck, you know they're already talking about money. The question is, are they learning the right things? Most aren't. They're picking up fragments—from TikTok influencers, peers, or family members who may not be in a position to teach sound financial habits. By stepping into the role of financial guide, even informally, you can help reshape the way your students view money. You can plant seeds that lead to long-term behavior change, even if your school doesn't offer a formal personal finance class.

One of the simplest but most powerful concepts to introduce is the idea of "paying yourself first." When students hear that phrase, it often sparks curiosity: "Wait, you mean before bills? Before spending on fun?" Exactly. Teaching them that even $5 from a birthday gift or a part-time job can go into savings first is transformational. It helps them see saving as an act of self-respect, not just something adults do when they "have extra." Framing it this way makes it emotionally resonant. It's about worth, not just math.

Budgeting, too, can be made relatable. You don't need a worksheet with fake expenses and a pretend salary. Start with a real-life challenge: "You have $50 to last the week. You want to eat out, buy a game, and save. What's your plan?" Give them scenarios that mirror their actual lives, not the hypothetical ones designed for generic curriculum. If your students are older, invite them to track their spending for one week. Just the act of observing can lead to smarter choices. It's like a fitness tracker for money—once you see it, you can't unsee it.

Debt is trickier. It can feel abstract to young people, especially those who haven't yet been offered a credit card or taken on a student loan. But you can start with analogies. For instance, explain interest as the "cost of renting money." If they borrow $100, they don't just owe $100 back—they owe more. That extra is the rent. And the longer they take to pay it back, the higher that rent gets. Break it down in a way that feels concrete. Tie it to their world: "If you buy a $500 gaming system on credit and don't pay it off quickly, it could cost you $700 or more." That hits differently than a vague warning about "bad credit."

Don't underestimate the power of stories. Share your own if you're comfortable—a financial mistake you made in college, a time you used a budget to get out of a tough spot, a win you had paying off debt. Students connect deeply with vulnerability and honesty, especially when it comes from someone they respect. They may not remember every tip you give them, but they'll remember the feeling of being seen and taught with care. And they'll carry that with them.

You can also empower students by showing them tools. Walk them through a simple app like Mint, YNAB, or a Google spreadsheet. Have them set a savings goal and check in each month. Encourage them to write out a "spending plan" instead of a budget—it feels less restrictive. The goal is to give them agency over their money instead of fear. If you have older students, explain how to compare debit vs. credit, or why checking your credit score matters. Bring in guest speakers, show real-life case studies, or use current events to spark discussion.

Some schools will push back. They'll say this isn't in the curriculum. Or that it's too controversial. But what's more controversial than sending kids into the world financially blind? This doesn't require a full semester course. It requires intention. A lesson here, a conversation there, a hallway chat that leads to a lightbulb moment. Start small. Consistency and repetition matter more than grandeur.

And if you want to make it a mission, go further. Propose a lunch-and-learn series. Start a personal finance elective. Partner with your school's counseling or career-readiness staff. Advocate for state policy changes that mandate financial literacy. Create a library of books or videos students can access on their own. Make this a part of your teaching legacy—because the students you reach may never forget who first taught them how money really works.

You don't have to be a financial advisor to teach these basics. You just have to be willing to start the conversation. As a teacher, you already have the trust and the platform. Now all you need is the intention. And if you keep it personal—if you make it about empowerment, not lectures—you'll be amazed at what your students take with them long after the bell rings.

Chapter 44: Creating a Generational Wealth Plan – Even If You Don't Think You Have One

Let's begin by dismantling a harmful myth: that only wealthy people create generational wealth. The truth is, you don't need to have a million-dollar estate or own investment properties in three zip codes to lay the foundation for financial continuity in your family. As a teacher, you are already creating generational wealth when you model budgeting, save for retirement, invest in your child's education, or have difficult conversations about money with your loved ones. This chapter isn't about chasing a dollar amount; it's about shifting how you view what you pass on. Wealth isn't just cash—it's wisdom, habits, financial tools, and preparedness. The impact of what you teach, show, and leave behind has the power to outlast your paycheck.

When we say "generational wealth," most people picture large inheritances. But for many educators, the most important wealth you pass down isn't monetary at all. It's the systems and principles you put in place. Do your children understand how insurance works? Do they know the value of compounding interest? Are they watching you live beneath your means, prioritize savings, and avoid unnecessary debt? If so, you're building a wealth legacy that will influence their decisions long after you're gone. Even if you never leave them a dime, you've given them something deeply valuable: the mindset and behaviors that build financial peace.

That said, if you *can* leave behind financial resources—even a modest sum—you have the chance to break cycles and rewrite futures. Teachers often underestimate the value of what they're accumulating. Between your pension, your 403(b), your Roth IRA, life insurance, and possibly home equity, you may be worth more on paper than you think. The key is organizing these pieces in a way that they continue working for your family even when you're not here to explain them. That means naming beneficiaries, updating wills, writing letters of instruction, and talking to your loved ones while you still can.

Start by reviewing your accounts. Who is the beneficiary on your pension? What about your 403(b) or any life insurance policies through work? Is your will current? Do your children or partner know how to access your important documents if something happened to you tomorrow? These aren't easy conversations, but they are the heart of legacy planning. Generational wealth isn't about waiting until you have more. It's about doing the best you can with what you already have, while you still have time to teach others how to handle it.

Also think about the education component. Could you write a letter to your children explaining your financial decisions and the values behind them? Could you leave instructions for how you want certain funds used—whether it's for college tuition, a home down payment, or building their own retirement accounts? A simple document like this can become a priceless compass. Combine that with a basic estate plan and you've done more than most Americans ever will.

You should also think about ownership and titling. Is your home titled in a way that it can pass smoothly to your spouse or children? Have you considered a transfer-on-death deed or a living trust if appropriate? These are conversations worth having with an estate planning attorney, especially if you're a homeowner. It's easy to assume things will just work out—but without legal clarity, even modest estates can cause major family stress.

Don't forget to include conversations around debt. Are you setting your kids up to avoid the same financial pitfalls you faced? Talk openly about credit cards, student loans, and lifestyle inflation. If your own parents never talked to you about money, you have a chance to do things differently. Show your kids your credit score. Let them sit in when you do the family budget. Normalize financial transparency. This is a part of your legacy, too.

You may also want to consider financial gifts you can give during your lifetime. Can you help your kids open a Roth IRA as soon as they start earning income? Can you co-sign a loan strategically (and carefully) to help them establish credit? Can you help them pay for a personal finance course, attend a workshop, or meet with a financial planner? Teaching them *how* to fish will always matter more than giving them the fish itself.

Remember, generational wealth planning is an ongoing process. You won't get it perfect. You'll forget a form here or miss an opportunity there. That's okay. What matters most is that you're trying—that you're intentional, open, and consistent. The fact that you're even reading this chapter puts you ahead of the curve. You're not just teaching your students. You're teaching your family. And that's a legacy worth fighting for.

Whether your estate totals $10,000 or $1 million, your plan matters. Even if no one else in your family has ever had these conversations, you can be the one to start. Quietly. Powerfully. Purposefully. You don't need anyone's permission to build a legacy—only the courage to begin mapping it out today.

Chapter 45: How to Prepare for Big Life Changes – Divorce, Marriage, Loss, or Relocation

Big life transitions don't just shift your emotional world—they affect your finances in ways that can ripple for decades. For teachers, these transitions can be particularly jarring because so much of your income, benefits, and retirement planning is tied to district policies, tenure timelines, union agreements, and local cost-of-living realities. When your life changes, your financial plan has to change with it—quickly and intelligently. Whether you're getting married, going through a divorce, moving districts, or grieving the death of a loved one, this chapter is about giving you the structure and emotional permission to plan for what happens next, even when your world feels unsteady.

Let's begin with marriage. Getting married can feel like a fairytale, but it's also a full-on merger of financial lives, obligations, and habits. You're not just saying "I do" to a person; you're also saying "I do" to their credit score, student loan balance, spending patterns, and financial mindset. For teachers marrying other educators, it becomes doubly important to understand how your pension systems interact, whether it's smarter to keep finances separate or join them, and how to build a household budget that respects both teaching incomes. This is a moment to map out how bills are paid, who contributes to retirement, how insurance is managed, and how long-term goals are defined.

Divorce, on the other hand, is one of the most financially devastating events a teacher can go through. If you've relied on shared income or taken time off to raise children, the financial recalibration is steep and often painful. Teachers must also be aware of what happens to their pension during divorce—in some states, a portion may be assigned to a former spouse. You'll need to revisit your beneficiaries, create or revise your estate plan, and ensure that your income and expenses are recalculated based on your new reality. This is not about fear; it's about knowing how to protect your future.

Grief and loss bring their own financial storms. The death of a spouse, parent, or close loved one can be paralyzing, and financial paperwork often feels cruelly out of place in moments of mourning. But it's essential to know how to access survivor benefits, update your will and power of attorney, and create a new financial plan that reflects your changed responsibilities. Teachers with dependents or aging parents should make sure their own wishes are clearly documented, with backup plans for care, income replacement, and housing stability.

Relocation can be an exciting fresh start or a tough sacrifice. Whether you're moving for a better district, to be closer to family, or because of personal circumstances, relocating can upend your entire financial structure. District salary schedules vary wildly by geography. A lateral move on paper might actually represent a step backward when local taxes, cost of living, and housing prices are factored in. This is also where vesting timelines matter: if you're just a year away from pension vesting in your current district, you need to weigh the long-term cost of leaving early. A smart relocation plan includes financial modeling, not just packing boxes.

Many teachers don't realize how dramatically their benefits can shift during big life events. Marriage might allow you to join a spouse's insurance plan—or remove you from subsidy eligibility. Divorce might mean COBRA coverage or a scramble to find your own plan. Death in the family could trigger life insurance payouts that need to be managed carefully, not spent emotionally. Moving may shift your eligibility for union protections or impact your retirement contributions. Knowing what to expect from HR, and what to ask for, puts you in control instead of in panic.

These transitions also affect your taxes. Marriage changes your filing status, deductions, and credit eligibility. Divorce might bring alimony or child support into play. Relocation can create multi-state tax confusion. Inheritance or insurance payouts can shift your tax bracket. Make sure to consult with a CPA or qualified tax advisor during any major life change. Teachers often underutilize professional financial help, but this is one of the times it can save you thousands and prevent years of regret.

Emotionally, these transitions often leave teachers feeling like they have to "stay strong" for others—students, staff, and even family. But your financial life deserves your full attention too. Create space to pause, reflect, and plan. Consider meeting with a financial planner, especially one familiar with teacher-specific benefits and retirement systems. You are not weak for needing help. You are wise for seeking clarity.

Every teacher should have a flexible financial plan that can adapt as life throws curveballs. That means more than a budget—it means understanding your insurance, keeping estate documents updated, knowing where your money goes each month, and checking in on your retirement trajectory. When big changes come, your plan should already have room to stretch.

This chapter isn't about expecting the worst—it's about being unshakable when life changes shape. Whether you're starting a new chapter or closing an old one, your financial literacy is the thread that helps you stay grounded, prepared, and fully present in the life you're building next.

Chapter 46: Avoiding Financial Burnout – Why Self-Care Includes Your Bank Account

Teaching is more than a job—it's a calling. But when the emotional labor, long hours, and financial strain pile up, even the most passionate educators can hit a wall. Financial burnout doesn't look the same for every teacher. For some, it shows up as resentment every time a paycheck falls short of covering essentials. For others, it's the quiet stress of mounting credit card debt or the gnawing anxiety of not being able to afford a vacation. At its core, financial burnout happens when your energy is spent faster than your income can support your needs—emotional, physical, and financial. And while many teachers think of self-care as bubble baths or a night off from grading, financial self-care is just as essential.

Let's be honest: financial burnout is often silent and normalized in education. It's the teacher who jokes about living on coffee and ramen, the colleague who skips doctor appointments because of a high deductible, or the mentor who delays retirement because they "can't afford to stop working." This normalization creates a dangerous narrative—that struggling is part of the profession, that it's noble to sacrifice everything for the job. But the truth is, no one can teach effectively when they're financially depleted. Recognizing the early signs of financial burnout is an act of self-preservation, not selfishness. And addressing it isn't about making six figures—it's about making sustainable decisions with the salary you do have.

One major contributor to burnout is the mismatch between a teacher's income and their growing financial responsibilities. Whether you're paying off student loans, supporting children, helping aging parents, or just trying to afford basic living expenses in a high-cost area, your paycheck is being pulled in too many directions. Teachers often feel stuck because their income is relatively fixed, while their needs and expenses fluctuate constantly. That tension—between limited income and expanding demands—is a slow drip of stress that can lead to burnout if not addressed with clarity and intention.

Another factor is guilt-driven spending. Teachers are nurturers by nature, and that extends to their wallets. How many times have you bought supplies for your classroom out of pocket? Or paid for a student's lunch? Or said yes to a fundraiser when you should've said no? While these actions come from a place of care, over time they chip away at your own financial well-being. One of the first steps in avoiding financial burnout is setting emotional boundaries around money. That means learning how to say no without guilt, and recognizing that your personal financial health is not selfish—it's foundational.

Budgeting can feel like a dirty word when you're already overwhelmed. But a thoughtful, values-based budget is one of the best antidotes to financial burnout. Rather than restricting joy, a good budget gives you permission. Permission to prioritize self-care. Permission to save for rest. Permission to say no. Start with a basic monthly breakdown: fixed expenses, minimum debt payments, savings goals, and spending money. Then take it a step further and align your spending with what actually brings you peace, not just convenience. Cut what drains you. Protect what restores you. Budgeting isn't about shame; it's about strategy.

Side hustles can help, but they can also hurt. Many teachers take on tutoring, coaching, or gig work to supplement their income. When done with intention, side income can ease financial strain. But when done out of desperation or without boundaries, it adds another layer of exhaustion. Before taking on extra work, ask yourself: Does this align with my strengths? Does it create breathing room or stress? Is the trade-off of time and energy worth the financial gain? Avoiding burnout means treating your time as a non-renewable resource—just like money.

Financial self-care also includes regular money check-ins. Once a month, sit down and look at your bank account, credit card balances, and savings. Not to judge yourself, but to stay awake at the wheel. Burnout thrives in avoidance. When you stop looking at your money, you stop steering your financial future. These check-ins can be short and simple. What came in? What went out? What can I adjust? Over time, these moments become less stressful and more empowering. You don't need to know everything, but you do need to stay engaged.

Part of healing financial burnout is giving yourself permission to rest without guilt. If you've been carrying financial stress for years, it's okay to be tired. It's okay to feel behind. But you're not behind. You're just now learning how to care for your financial self with the same compassion you give your students. That starts with acknowledging how hard it's been, and then slowly rewriting the story. You are allowed to rest. You are allowed to rebuild. You are allowed to restructure your relationship with money.

Boundaries are your burnout shield. Boundaries with spending. Boundaries with how much you give. Boundaries with how much you work. Say no more often. Reassess subscriptions. Stop covering for school districts that should be funding their own supplies. Practice saying, "I wish I could, but it's not in my budget right now." Every time you protect your financial peace, you protect your emotional health. And every time you say no to something that depletes you, you're saying yes to long-term sustainability.

Avoiding financial burnout isn't about becoming rich. It's about becoming resilient. It's about making money decisions that honor your energy, your values, and your vision for a balanced life. You don't need more spreadsheets. You need more compassion—for yourself, for the hard choices you've made, and for the new ones you're learning to make. Self-care isn't a luxury. It's a financial necessity. And your bank account deserves just as much care as your classroom.

Not every financial struggle has a quick fix, but every burnout cycle has an exit ramp. The key is seeing it, stepping off slowly, and walking toward something healthier—one decision, one boundary, one breath at a time.

Chapter 47: Staying Sharp – Ongoing Financial Education for Lifelong Educators

The same way educators commit to professional development for their craft, the journey of financial literacy also demands continual growth. Financial education is not a one-and-done seminar or a weekend webinar; it's a living, breathing practice that evolves with your life. Whether you're entering your 30th year in the classroom or navigating your first, your financial needs, responsibilities, and opportunities shift constantly. Staying financially sharp means being willing to revisit what you think you know, update your assumptions, and continue learning.

For many teachers, the concept of financial literacy feels like something reserved for Wall Street types or high-income earners, not people drawing a public school salary. That mindset is part of the problem. Financial education isn't about wealth—it's about clarity, agency, and peace of mind. Just as you wouldn't ignore new curriculum standards or teaching tools, you can't afford to ignore changes in tax law, retirement rules, student loan reforms, and investment opportunities. Teachers deserve to stay current, because your financial life is just as worthy of expertise and support as your classroom.

Your district might offer access to a 403(b), a pension plan, or financial wellness webinars, but many teachers aren't fully taking advantage of these benefits simply because no one ever taught them how. That needs to change. Continuing your financial education doesn't mean you need to become a finance professional. It just means taking steps to understand what applies to you—and how to use it. Consider attending a seminar through your union, setting up a monthly money-check session with fellow teachers, or subscribing to a personal finance podcast that actually speaks your language.

Being proactive matters. Too many educators wait until a crisis—divorce, death, job change, or debt collection—before learning the basics of money management. But ongoing financial education is preventive care. It's the same as attending a health screening or doing a classroom observation. It keeps you aware. It helps you spot problems early. And it gives you more time to make informed decisions instead of panicked ones. Knowing how your pension works or how to set up an HSA isn't extra credit—it's essential knowledge.

Let's be honest: the financial world can feel deliberately confusing. Terms like "indexed annuity" or "income laddering" weren't designed with teachers in mind. But that doesn't mean they're beyond your understanding. In fact, educators are some of the best-positioned people to grasp complex topics—because you do it every day for your students. Approach financial literacy the same way you approach a new subject area: with curiosity, patience, and a willingness to learn from mistakes. That mindset builds financial confidence over time.

Technology has made it easier than ever to continue your financial education. From free YouTube channels and online classes to budget tracking apps and robo-advisors, you don't have to do this alone. Even if you only dedicate one hour a month to improving your financial knowledge, that's still 12 hours a year—and that adds up. Ask yourself: how much time did you spend last year understanding your money? If the answer is close to zero, start small. No guilt. Just momentum.

Professional development funds are often underutilized for personal finance workshops. If your district allows it, propose a session focused on retirement planning, debt reduction, or even estate basics. Teachers sharing what they've learned with other teachers is powerful. You know the context. You understand the limitations. And you can tailor strategies in a way that actually resonates. Your financial journey isn't a side project—it's part of your professional path.

Just like curriculum changes, life changes too. Your financial needs at 25 will be wildly different from your needs at 55. Kids, marriages, relocations, illnesses, inheritances, and career changes can all force you to update your financial game plan. Ongoing education gives you the resilience to adapt. The longer you teach, the more you understand that being prepared isn't about having all the answers—it's about being equipped to ask better questions.

As an educator, you already have the tools: the capacity to learn, the humility to grow, and the resilience to try again. Financial literacy honors those same skills. It's not just about building wealth—it's about building clarity. As your career unfolds, make a habit of checking in with yourself financially, just like you do professionally. The same diligence you bring to your classroom deserves to be brought to your life.

Let this chapter be your reminder that you don't need to wait for a financial emergency to start learning. You can start now, wherever you are, with what you have. One article, one podcast, one conversation at a time. That's how lifelong learners become financially powerful. And if anyone can model that kind of growth, it's a teacher.

Chapter 48: From Classroom to Community Leader – Advocating for Financial Literacy in Schools

In every school building, there are leaders who don't wear administrative titles. They are teachers who quietly shape not only lessons, but lives. If you're reading this chapter, you may be one of them—someone who has mastered the art of educating hearts and minds and now feels called to do something more. Something bigger. Advocating for financial literacy in your school, your district, or your community might not have been in your original job description. But it's a role you were born to play, and the impact can be generational. It begins with the decision to speak up, to propose a change, and to help students learn not only how to earn a living, but how to manage one.

Many teachers avoid the topic of money altogether, feeling unqualified or worried they'll say the wrong thing. But financial literacy doesn't require perfection. It requires permission—permission to tell the truth about what students will face, to share what you've learned, and to open doors for young people to avoid common mistakes. Students don't need a flawless financial expert. They need a relatable adult who will guide them, model transparency, and introduce them to tools they've never seen before. If you've ever explained the difference between a need and a want to a kindergartner or helped a high schooler fill out their FAFSA, you've already begun the work.

Start with your classroom. Can you integrate personal finance examples into math word problems? Can your social studies curriculum include historical movements that shaped economic systems and inequality? Can you make space for a discussion during advisory or homeroom about budgeting, college costs, or even credit scores? Advocacy doesn't always require a grant or a board meeting. Sometimes, it starts with a sidebar conversation after class that changes how a student views money for the rest of their life.

That said, systemic change often requires systemic action. If your school lacks a financial literacy curriculum, bring the topic to your department chair, principal, or PTA. Show them why it matters. Share statistics. Connect it to student outcomes, college readiness, or career education. Align your argument with your school's existing priorities. Ask for pilot programs, guest speakers, professional development, or a designated financial literacy week. Don't be afraid to lead from where you stand.

You might feel like you're going against the grain. You might get pushback. Budget constraints, standardized testing, and curriculum overload are real barriers. But remember, advocating for financial literacy is not an add-on. It's a foundation. Students who understand financial basics are more focused, less stressed, and better prepared for adulthood. Your efforts to teach them about saving, credit, loans, and investing may be the difference between years of hardship and a lifetime of stability.

Consider collaboration. Are there colleagues in your building who are equally passionate? Could the math department, business electives, and school counselors create a team to develop consistent financial messaging across grades? Could your students interview local entrepreneurs, participate in mock budgeting challenges, or hear from alumni who navigated student debt? Advocacy thrives in community. You don't have to do this alone.

Your credibility matters. You don't need a finance degree to lead. Your lived experience—as a working adult, a parent, a borrower, a saver—is a curriculum in itself. When you share how you planned for your first home, paid off a car, or saved for retirement on a teacher's salary, you are giving students something no textbook can: context. And when they see a teacher they respect model responsible financial choices, they remember it.

Over time, your influence may stretch beyond your school walls. Maybe you'll speak at a community event, join a state task force, or help shape district policy. Maybe you'll mentor other educators who want to bring this topic into their classrooms. Maybe you'll even co-create a local scholarship, teach a summer money boot camp, or help establish a credit union partnership for your students. Each step you take normalizes the idea that teachers are not only knowledge-givers, but financial literacy leaders.

Remember, the work will look different in every school. What matters is that you begin. Start where you are, use what you have, and teach what you know. The ripple effects of one teacher advocating for financial literacy can stretch across generations, communities, and systems. And it all begins with a voice—yours.

Some chapters in this book end with a checklist or reflection. This one ends with a reminder: you are more powerful than you think, and your leadership in this area is not only possible—it's necessary.

Chapter 49: Final Chapter: You Educate the World – Now It's Time to Master Your Own Money Story

You have spent your career investing in others—their potential, their growth, their futures. You've taught kids how to read, calculate, think critically, and believe in themselves. You've stepped into classrooms that didn't have enough supplies, where the heating didn't work, or where behavior issues consumed more energy than the lesson plans themselves. And you still showed up. You still taught. And you still gave more of yourself than most people ever will. But now it's time to turn some of that care, attention, and devotion inward. This is the moment you begin to rewrite your own money story—not out of guilt or fear, but out of strength, clarity, and self-respect.

For so many educators, financial literacy has felt like an outside world—one that belonged to business majors or investors, not teachers. Maybe it was dismissed as irrelevant during college. Maybe it was just too overwhelming to tackle while managing lesson plans, grading, and everything else life demanded. But here's the truth: financial literacy belongs to you. The numbers matter, yes. But what matters more is how those numbers make you feel. Are you waking up with peace of mind or constant low-grade anxiety about money? Are you teaching during the day and losing sleep at night over student loans, credit card balances, or an unclear retirement plan? That's not sustainable. That's not fair. And that's not your fault. But it is your moment to change it.

This book has taken you through the journey of your teaching career—from your first paycheck to your final year in the classroom. We've explored how to stretch a budget, build credit, protect your income, and understand complex benefits systems like pensions and 403(b)s. We've looked at how to buy a home on a teacher's salary, how to support kids without draining your future, and how to plan for retirement with confidence rather than confusion. But now we're going to talk about something deeper: how to *own* your financial identity. Because numbers only get you so far. The rest is mindset, behavior, and belief.

Owning your money story starts with forgiving yourself for not knowing what no one taught you. If you've ever felt ashamed about a credit card balance or anxious about not having an emergency fund, pause and take a breath. You were surviving. You were doing what you had to do. And now, you're choosing to learn. That makes you brave. That makes you powerful. Your new financial story doesn't have to be perfect. It just has to be yours—intentional, informed, and flexible enough to grow with you.

Take a look at where you are right now. What do you own? What do you owe? What do you understand, and what still confuses you? Create a money snapshot. Don't judge it. Don't panic. Just observe it. This is your starting line—not your finish line. From here, you can create a plan. Not a Pinterest-perfect financial plan. A real one. Maybe you decide to finally open that Roth IRA. Maybe you call HR and ask how your pension actually works. Maybe you and your partner sit down and have a financial check-in that's been avoided for too long. These are the things that shift your life. Quietly. Powerfully. One step at a time.

Understand that your money life is not separate from your emotional life. They are deeply connected. Every dollar you spend, save, or avoid has a story behind it—a fear, a memory, a hope. That's why money is never just about math. It's about what we think we deserve. And too many teachers have been taught, implicitly or explicitly, that their financial lives come second. That self-sacrifice is noble. That struggling is normal. It's not. You deserve to thrive. You deserve to feel ease. And you can still be generous and selfless without neglecting your future.

Your future, by the way, is not something far away. It's being written right now. Every decision you make—big or small—adds up. Whether it's skipping takeout one night a week to put money into savings or finally updating your beneficiaries, it all matters. It all counts. No effort is too small. No action is wasted. And even if you've made mistakes in the past (who hasn't?), that doesn't disqualify you from financial stability or wealth-building. It just means you're human. And like any good teacher, you can learn. You can adapt. You can teach yourself new rules.

As you move forward, start thinking about legacy. Not in a grand, philosophical way (unless you want to), but in a practical, grounded way. What do you want your money to do for your family? Your students? Your community? Do you want to leave something behind? Fund scholarships? Help your children buy their first home? Retire with the freedom to volunteer, travel, or mentor new teachers? These are not pipe dreams. These are plans you can make, even if they shift over time. Legacy is not about how much you leave behind—it's about how intentionally you lived with what you had.

So let this be the chapter where you look in the mirror and say: I have the right to understand money. I have the right to make financial decisions without fear or shame. I have the right to learn at my own pace. I have the right to rewrite the story I've been told about teachers and money. And I'm not doing it alone. I'm doing it with a community of educators who are stepping into their power together. One lesson, one choice, one paycheck at a time.

This book may be ending, but your journey is not. It's just getting clearer. It's getting stronger. And whether you're just starting out or wrapping up your career, you now have tools, language, and strategies that no one can take away from you. You've spent a lifetime preparing others for the future. Now it's your turn.

Disclaimers

Financial Literacy for Teachers was written to educate, empower, and support educators in building financial clarity, stability, and long-term confidence. The insights shared here are drawn from my years of experience as a wealth manager working with real teachers—many of whom have faced unique financial challenges despite being highly educated, hardworking, and deeply mission-driven. This book is not theory—it's based on practical strategies and real conversations with teachers navigating life both inside and outside the classroom.

That said, it's important to understand what this book **is**, and what it **is not**.

This Book Is for Educational Purposes Only

All content in *Financial Literacy for Teachers* is provided solely for educational and informational purposes. It is meant to introduce teachers and educators to important financial principles—from budgeting on a teacher's salary to understanding pension benefits, navigating student loan repayment, saving for retirement, and setting boundaries with financial requests from family or school communities.

While the book includes helpful examples, frameworks, and planning ideas, it does **not** constitute personalized financial advice. Every teacher's situation is different. Your district pay scale, your benefits package, your family responsibilities, your debt, your retirement goals—all of these require a personalized plan.

Before making significant financial decisions—including those related to investments, taxes, insurance, or estate planning—you should consult licensed professionals who understand your specific circumstances.

This Book Does Not Offer Legal Advice

Some of the content in this book may mention legal topics—such as wills, powers of attorney, insurance beneficiary designations, or estate planning basics. However, this book is **not** intended to be legal advice and should not be used as a substitute for working with a qualified attorney.

If you are:

- Drafting or updating a will or healthcare proxy
- Naming beneficiaries for retirement or life insurance plans
- Thinking about guardianship for your children
- Setting up a trust for family or charitable purposes

...please consult a licensed attorney in your state. Legal strategies vary widely by jurisdiction, and it's important to receive advice tailored to your personal needs and legal obligations.

This Book Is Not Financial or Investment Advice

You'll find chapters on 403(b) plans, Roth IRAs, pensions, saving strategies, credit use, and managing debt. These are vital parts of a teacher's financial life—but nothing in this book is a recommendation to invest or not invest in any specific asset or strategy.

I am a wealth manager by trade, but this book is not delivered under a financial advisory contract. It's an educational tool—not a substitute for working directly with a financial planner or advisor.

If you are:

- Choosing between a 403(b) and 457(b)
- Evaluating an annuity product
- Considering buying a home on a teacher's income

- Planning when to take your pension

...please work with a qualified financial advisor or fiduciary planner, especially one who understands educator compensation structures and retirement plans.

This Book Does Not Provide Tax or Accounting Advice

Taxes matter deeply to teachers—whether you're managing student loan interest deductions, optimizing your educator expense deduction, or figuring out how retirement withdrawals will be taxed. But this book is **not** tax advice, nor am I a CPA.

If you are:

- Filing taxes with multiple income sources (e.g., summer jobs or tutoring)
- Claiming educator deductions or education-related credits
- Evaluating whether to file jointly or separately during a divorce
- Navigating income-driven repayment or public service loan forgiveness (PSLF)

...you should work with a tax professional. Preferably one who understands how educator tax benefits, state pensions, and student loans intersect.

This Book Offers No Guarantees

Reading this book will not guarantee that you become debt-free, financially independent, or ready for retirement by age 55. The goal of this book is **not perfection**—it's progress.

The stories, examples, and scenarios shared here are for educational purposes. They are not predictions. Your financial success will depend on your habits, your decisions, your opportunities, and your support network. Your path may include obstacles beyond your control—health issues, life events, inflation, or job changes.

This book gives you tools. But the journey is yours.

Your Responsibility, Your Outcomes

By reading this book, you agree that I, Pat Brown, MBA — and any affiliated platforms such as FinancialLiteracyForNIL.com or FinancialLiteracyForTeachers.com — am not liable for the financial outcomes of your personal decisions. I am sharing insights based on my experience and work with educators, but I am not responsible for individual tax filings, investment losses, missed savings targets, or estate disputes.

You are your own best advocate. And while you deserve a team of support, you remain responsible for your financial decisions.

Build a Team That Understands You

Most teachers are used to being self-reliant. But you don't have to figure everything out on your own. Over time, you may benefit from working with:

- A tax professional who understands educator-specific deductions and PSLF
- A financial advisor who respects your values and works in your best interest
- An attorney who can draft a will, guardianship instructions, or other legal documents
- An insurance professional who can help you evaluate disability or life coverage
- A student loan specialist who understands forgiveness programs

This book is meant to supplement—not replace—that team. If you don't have professionals you trust, start building your bench. It's never too early.

You've worked hard for your salary, your pension credits, your benefits, and your peace of mind. Now let's make sure you're protecting that investment, understanding your options, and planning for the future with intention.

Because you deserve to teach from a place of strength—not stress. Let's build a plan that honors that.

Coordinating Your Financial Life as an Educator: Why Integration Matters

Coordinating Your Financial Life as an Educator: Why Integration Matters

Managing your money as a teacher isn't just about budgeting or saving for retirement—it's about building a coordinated system that supports your values, protects your income, and prepares you for the future. Financial security for educators rarely comes from one big windfall. Instead, it comes from years of intentional choices that align across your salary, benefits, pension, taxes, insurance, investments, and estate plan.

Done right, this kind of planning turns complexity into clarity and transforms the stress of "getting by" into the confidence of building a legacy—however big or small.

Your Financial Life Is Interconnected

Most teachers juggle multiple responsibilities—family, classrooms, grading, side gigs, student loans, and more. And yet, their financial planning often happens in disconnected silos: a retirement account here, a tax return there, an insurance policy they forgot they had.

The truth is, your financial success doesn't hinge on one good year or one perfect investment. It comes from making all the parts of your financial life work in harmony. When your pension planning connects with your tax strategy, when your estate plan aligns with your insurance, when your investments reflect your values—you move from financial survival to financial strategy.

Let's walk through what that integrated approach looks like for educators.

1. Estate Planning Isn't Just for the Wealthy

If you have children, own a home, or want your assets passed on in a certain way, you need a will—and possibly more. Even modest assets can cause stress, confusion, or legal issues for your loved ones if left unplanned.

Action Step: Create or update your will. Name guardians if you have kids. Review your life insurance and retirement account beneficiaries to ensure they reflect your wishes. If you're part of a pension system, make sure your survivor benefits are aligned with your broader plan.

2. Tax Planning Shouldn't Be a Once-a-Year Event

Many educators miss tax-saving opportunities simply because no one ever showed them how to plan ahead. Whether it's deducting out-of-pocket classroom expenses, qualifying for the educator tax credit, or timing contributions to a 403(b) or Roth IRA, proactive tax planning can make a major difference.

Pros: You keep more of what you earn.

Cons: It requires planning ahead and possibly professional help.

Action Step: Sit down mid-year with a tax professional or advisor. Review your withholding, assess upcoming deductions, and develop a long-term strategy for tax-efficient savings.

3. Insurance Isn't Just a Contract—It's a Safety Net

Too often, teachers are underinsured—or overpaying for the wrong kinds of coverage. Life insurance, disability insurance, and even umbrella coverage can play a crucial role in protecting your income and your family's future.

Real-Life Example: A teacher who became unexpectedly disabled had long-term disability coverage that paid only a fraction of her salary—forcing her family into financial hardship. A better policy (and earlier review) could have protected her income fully.

Action Step: Conduct a full insurance audit. What would happen to your income, savings, or dependents if something unexpected occurred tomorrow?

4. Investing Isn't About Picking Stocks—It's About Long-Term Goals

Many teachers have access to retirement plans like a 403(b), 457(b), or a state pension—but few know how to make the most of them. Without guidance, they may invest too conservatively, miss tax-deferred growth opportunities, or forget to account for inflation in their long-term plans.

Action Step: Build or revise your investment policy. Know what you're investing for (retirement, college, travel, etc.), and match your risk level and timelines accordingly. Don't just default to the "safe" option—make sure it's also smart.

5. When You Have a Side Hustle, Know How to Treat It Like a Business

Whether it's tutoring, coaching, selling curriculum, or summer work, many educators have additional income streams. But that money needs to be tracked, taxed, and optimized just like your classroom income.

Real-Life Example: A teacher earned $12,000 tutoring over the summer but didn't set aside taxes—and ended up with a surprise bill. Another teacher turned a small Etsy shop into a thriving side business by treating it like a real enterprise with proper budgeting, taxes, and reinvestment.

Action Step: Keep separate accounts for side income. Track expenses. Consider forming an LLC or sole proprietorship if your earnings grow. Meet with a tax advisor who understands small businesses and educators.

6. Don't Wait Until Retirement to Think About Liquidity

If you're counting on your pension or retirement plan to carry you through retirement, think again. Many teachers retire only to realize they need access to liquid funds—to travel, care for family, or cover rising costs. Liquidity planning means having money that's accessible when you need it—not just "on paper."

Action Step: Start a liquid savings plan now. Build up a "retirement bridge fund" to cover the years between retirement and full pension/social security payouts. Don't rely solely on locked-away funds.

7. Philanthropy Isn't Just About Writing Checks—It's About Living Your Values

Educators are often deeply generous people. Whether you give to your school, your church, a local cause, or your former students, giving back should be a part of your financial plan—not an afterthought.

Action Step: Create a charitable giving plan. Determine how much you want to give annually. Consider donor-advised funds, gifting appreciated assets, or legacy gifts in your will to maximize your impact.

8. The Key to Teacher Wealth? Coordination, Not Perfection

You don't need to master every financial topic. But you do need a system—a rhythm—where the different parts of your financial life talk to each other.

Real-Life Scenario: A married couple—both public school teachers—coordinated their pensions, savings, and insurance to retire at 58, travel full-time for two years, and return to part-time teaching by choice. They weren't "rich." They were just organized and intentional.

Action Step: Make a list of your professionals: CPA, financial advisor, attorney, HR rep, insurance agent. Are they talking to each other? Are you getting coordinated advice—or piecemeal plans?

Final Word: You're Not Just Managing a Budget—You're Leading a Legacy

Teachers shape minds and futures every day. You deserve a financial plan that reflects the same care and intentionality you give your students.

Managing your finances is not about chasing wealth—it's about designing a life of security, purpose, and peace. That only happens when all the pieces fit together.

If you need deeper guidance on how to align your pension, taxes, estate plan, savings goals, and side income, don't hesitate to build a team around you. Your financial future deserves as much planning as your classroom.

This book is your first step toward building that kind of life—with confidence, clarity, and leadership.

Financial Literacy Is Powerful — But Only If You Act On It

Understanding money is one thing. Using that understanding to make real-life, strategic decisions — that's where transformation happens.

As a teacher, your financial future will not be shaped by a single lucky break or a perfect retirement plan. It will be the result of many small, intentional actions — setting up the right accounts, choosing the right benefits, planning for the next chapter, and protecting what you've worked so hard to earn.

You don't need to know everything. But you do need to *do* something.

The following checklist is designed to help you move from understanding to execution — from theory to financial traction — right where you are.

1. Start With a Full Review of Your Financial Picture

Before you can make progress, you need a clear, honest view of where you stand.

- What's your monthly take-home pay?
- Are you tracking your spending?
- Do you know how much debt you owe — and at what interest rates?
- How much do you have saved for emergencies?
- Are your pension, 403(b), and/or Roth IRA on track to support your retirement timeline?

Action Step: Create or revisit a one-page financial snapshot. Include income, expenses, debts, savings, benefits, and insurance. If you have a partner, do this together. Clarity is the first step toward confidence.

2. Understand Your Retirement System

Many teachers rely heavily on their pension — but few understand how it works.

- How long do you need to teach to become vested?
- What will your monthly payout be at different retirement ages?
- Should you also contribute to a 403(b), Roth IRA, or both?
- What happens if you switch states or leave teaching altogether?

Action Step: Log in to your state retirement portal and print your most recent benefit statement. Schedule a meeting with HR or a financial advisor to review your pension and ask how to supplement it wisely.

3. Build a Realistic Emergency Fund

You don't need six figures saved to feel secure — but you do need access to cash when life surprises you.

- How many months of expenses do you have saved?
- Is it in a high-yield savings account, not just your checking account?
- What would happen if your car needed $2,000 of repairs next week?

Action Step: Set up automatic transfers of $25–$100 a week to a dedicated savings account until you reach three to six months of basic expenses.

4. Make a Plan to Eliminate High-Interest Debt

Credit cards, personal loans, or old private student loans can quietly drain your finances.

Action Step: List every debt you have, from highest interest rate to lowest.

Focus on paying off the highest-interest ones first while making minimum payments on the rest. Use any side income, bonuses, or tax refunds to speed up the process.

5. Maximize Your Benefits

Your school district may offer more than you realize.

- Are you enrolled in the best health plan for your family?
- Are you contributing to a Flexible Spending Account (FSA) or Health Savings Account (HSA)?
- Do you have access to disability insurance or a group legal plan?
- Are you using any matching contributions on retirement plans?

Action Step: Ask HR for a full summary of your benefits. Schedule 30 minutes to review each section and decide what changes or enrollments you may have missed.

6. Create an Investment Strategy — Even If You're Not a Finance Nerd

Investing isn't gambling or trying to "beat the market." It's about time, consistency, and avoiding unnecessary fees.

Action Step: If you haven't already, open a Roth IRA (or start contributing to your 403(b)). Choose a target-date retirement fund or a low-cost index fund. Set it and forget it — but revisit once a year to check in.

7. Review Your Insurance Like It's a Financial Plan — Because It Is

Many teachers are underinsured without realizing it.

- Do you have enough term life insurance to protect your family if something happened?

- If you got hurt and couldn't work for six months, would you have disability coverage?
- Do you have umbrella insurance to cover lawsuits or large accidents?

Action Step: Print out your insurance policies. Highlight the coverage amounts. Then ask: If something major happened tomorrow, would this be enough?

8. Start Planning for Long-Term Goals Now — Even If They Feel Far Off

Whether it's buying a home, putting your kids through college, retiring early, or traveling the world after you leave the classroom — these things don't happen accidentally.

Action Step: Pick one big goal. Write it down. Estimate what it will cost. Then reverse engineer: how much would you need to save each month to reach it in 5, 10, or 20 years? Start with $50/month if that's all you can manage. Progress matters more than perfection.

9. Assemble a Support Team — Even If It's Just One Person to Start

You don't have to do all of this alone. A good advisor, accountant, or mentor can help you go further, faster.

Action Step: Find one trusted financial professional (fee-only advisor, CPA, credit counselor, etc.) who has experience working with educators. Even one annual check-in can change your financial trajectory.

10. Review Your Financial Plan Every Quarter

Just like your lesson plans adapt throughout the school year, your financial plan needs regular review.

Action Step: Put four dates on your calendar each year to sit down (solo or with your partner) and review your money: spending, saving, investing, protecting. Ask: What's working? What's not? What needs to change?

Final Word

You don't need to have a six-figure income to build wealth.

You don't need to be perfect to make progress.

You just need to take the next step — and then the one after that.

Financial literacy is powerful — but only if you act on it. For teachers, it's not just about making your money work harder. It's about reducing stress, protecting your peace, and creating a life that reflects the same intention and care you bring to your students.

Start where you are. Take small steps. Make it personal. And keep going.

Your future self will thank you.

Should You Manage Your Finances Alone or Work With a Professional?

At some point in your financial journey — especially as your income, savings, or family responsibilities grow — you'll face this critical question:

Should I keep managing my money myself, or should I bring in a professional?

For teachers, who are used to doing a lot with a little, the instinct is often to DIY everything — from budgeting and investing to tax filing and retirement planning. After all, you've been resourceful your whole career. You're smart, disciplined, and capable.

But as your financial life becomes more layered — pensions, 403(b)s, student loans, home ownership, estate planning, kids, long-term care — the decision becomes less about capability and more about **bandwidth, expertise, and peace of mind**.

1. Time Is a Real Cost

Managing your own finances takes more time than most people expect. There's tracking, researching, comparing options, making decisions, fixing mistakes, and keeping up with laws and benefits that change regularly.

Action Step: Ask yourself honestly: How many hours per month do I want to spend managing my finances? Would I rather spend that time doing what I love — teaching, resting, traveling, being with family — and let a trusted expert help with the financial load?

2. Complexity Adds Up Fast

Between student loan repayment options, navigating multiple retirement accounts, tracking pension vesting, choosing the right insurance policies, and eventually planning for Social Security and Medicare — it's a lot.

Real-Life Scenario: A mid-career teacher with multiple 403(b) accounts, private student loans, and a side business tutoring realized she was leaving money on the table and not investing effectively. After working with a planner, she consolidated her accounts, maximized tax benefits, and created a plan to pay off debt and fund her dream to buy a home.

Action Step: Map your financial life. If it includes more than 3–4 major pieces (debt, savings, retirement, dependents, property, insurance), it may be time to consider guidance.

3. Emotions Can Get in the Way

When you've worked hard for every dollar, it's easy to make money decisions based on fear or attachment — not strategy. A professional can help you take the emotion out of financial decisions and focus on facts and goals.

Pros: Clarity, objectivity, and decision-making based on your values and long-term success.

Cons: You may need to get used to trusting someone else with sensitive details. That's why fit matters.

Action Step: Make a list of financial decisions you've delayed or second-guessed. Would a third party with no emotional ties have helped you move forward more confidently?

4. Access to Better Tools and Opportunities

Financial advisors and planners often have access to tools, platforms, and opportunities that aren't available to the average person — including investment options, tax-advantaged strategies, or group insurance coverage.

Real-Life Scenario: A group of teachers pooled together to work with a financial advisor who helped them create a group 403(b) strategy with lower fees and clearer investment options. Together, they built more savings than they would have going it alone.

Action Step: Ask: What opportunities, tax breaks, or long-term strategies am I missing because I don't know what I don't know?

5. Tax Planning and Loan Repayment Require Strategy

Teachers often qualify for tax credits, student loan forgiveness, or educator deductions — but many miss out because they don't know how to plan ahead or optimize timing.

Action Step: Meet with a tax professional or certified financial planner who works with educators. They can help you avoid common filing mistakes, lower your tax bill, and help you decide which repayment plan or forgiveness program fits your goals.

6. Insurance, Estate Planning, and Retirement Need to Work Together

It's not just about saving for retirement — it's about making sure your whole financial house is protected. That means:

- Having the right life and disability insurance
- Setting up a basic will or trust
- Knowing what happens to your pension if you pass away
- Coordinating your insurance, retirement, and estate planning for maximum protection

Action Step: Schedule a "financial protection checkup." Even if you don't hire a professional full-time, a one-time consultation could save your family significant stress and money later.

7. Cost Is Real — But So Is Value

Yes, professionals charge fees. But so does doing it alone when you miss tax breaks, overpay interest, choose the wrong benefits, or stay stuck in financial uncertainty.

Pros: Coordinated strategy, saved time, less stress, better results.

Cons: Cost — but one that may pay for itself many times over.

Action Step: Don't just ask "What does it cost?" Ask: "What could I gain by having a trusted advisor in my corner?"

Final Word: Know When It's Time to Ask for Help

This book is designed to help you become confident and financially informed. But financial literacy isn't about doing everything alone. It's about making smart decisions — including when to call in support.

Some teachers love managing their money on their own. Others love the freedom that comes with handing the planning to someone they trust.

There is no shame in asking for help — only strength in knowing when it's time.

If you're ready to build a coordinated plan — for your money, your goals, your classroom life, and your retirement — there are professionals out there who specialize in helping teachers just like you.

You don't have to do it all. You just have to do what matters most.

And sometimes, the best investment you can make — is in guidance.

A Month-by-Month Financial Planning Guide for Teachers

Managing your finances as an educator isn't just about tracking spending or saving for retirement — it's about being intentional with your calendar, aligned with your goals, and proactive rather than reactive.

Whether you're early in your career or preparing to retire, this month-by-month guide helps teachers stay organized and empowered through every season of the school year and financial year. Consider this your blueprint for building wealth with confidence and consistency.

JANUARY

New Year, New Limits.

- Retirement plan contribution limits (403(b), 457, IRA) reset — increase or automate contributions.
- Update your W-4 if your family situation changed (marriage, new child, divorce).
- Review your personal and household budget based on your academic calendar and contract schedule.
- Begin collecting tax documents and checking on any educator-related deductions (e.g., classroom expenses).
- **Action Step:** Set one savings goal for the year and automate monthly transfers toward it.

FEBRUARY

Tax Prep and Organization.

- By early February, W-2s and 1099s should be in hand.
- Gather receipts for classroom purchases and professional development.
- Begin filling out your taxes or schedule with a professional.
- Review your credit report for accuracy.
- **Action Step:** Organize a tax folder (digital or physical) to track deductions specific to educators.

MARCH

Mid-Semester Money Check.

- File taxes early if you expect a refund — consider using it for debt reduction or savings.
- Review any side income (tutoring, summer work) and plan how to report and allocate it.
- Check on union benefits, educator discounts, and classroom reimbursements you may be missing.
- **Action Step:** Adjust your budget based on any tax return or updated expenses.

APRIL

Tax Deadline & Retirement Contributions.

- April 15 is the deadline to file federal taxes.
- Last chance to contribute to your IRA or HSA for the previous tax year.
- If age 73 or older, take your RMD (Required Minimum Distribution).
- **Action Step:** If you received a tax refund, split it: save part, invest part, and treat yourself modestly.

MAY

Home, Property, and Education Funding.

- Review property tax assessments and appeal if needed.
- May 29 (5/29 Day) is a reminder to contribute to a 529 college savings plan if you're funding education for a child or grandchild.
- Begin planning for summer spending or additional income.
- **Action Step:** Set a summer financial goal — saving, paying off debt, or increasing investments.

JUNE

Mid-Year Review.

- Teachers often receive lump sums or final paychecks — review your cash flow and savings allocation.
- Rebalance retirement accounts and reassess risk tolerance.
- Review charitable giving and start planning year-end donations.
- **Action Step:** Schedule a mid-year money meeting — even if it's just with yourself — to recalibrate.

JULY

Summer Strategy Session.

- Audit your year-to-date spending and saving.
- Explore extra income opportunities (summer school, tutoring, curriculum development).
- If retiring soon, begin gathering pension estimates and Social Security statements.
- **Action Step:** Review your beneficiary designations on all retirement and insurance accounts.

AUGUST

Back-to-School Budgeting.

- Set limits and priorities for classroom setup and supplies.
- Update or open a Flexible Spending Account (FSA) if available.
- Review and update insurance policies (health, disability, life).
- **Action Step:** Set a monthly "sinking fund" for next summer's needs — save now, breathe later.

SEPTEMBER

Open Enrollment Season Starts.

- Begin comparing health insurance plans, especially if you have new medical needs.
- Consider adjusting contributions to retirement accounts if your district allows it.
- Start thinking about year-end tax moves (donations, Roth conversions, etc.).
- **Action Step:** List all your benefits (including through your union) — many teachers don't use half of what's available.

OCTOBER

Finalize Your Benefits.

- October 15 is the tax deadline if you filed an extension.
- Review Open Enrollment elections — benefits, retirement contributions, vision, dental.
- Evaluate dependent care options and FSA contributions.
- **Action Step:** Confirm that your healthcare and insurance align with your family's current needs.

NOVEMBER

Plan for Giving & Gifting.

- Make charitable donations before year-end to claim deductions.
- Consider year-end tax moves: Roth conversions, harvesting investment losses, increasing 403(b) contributions.
- Reflect on your financial progress and write down 3 money goals for next year.
- **Action Step:** Contribute to educator-specific causes or education-focused charities — make giving part of your legacy.

DECEMBER

Finish Strong.

- Make final 403(b)/457 contributions before the end of the year.
- Complete any charitable giving, FSA spending, and required distributions.
- Review your net worth statement and overall financial plan.
- Revisit wills, estate documents, and beneficiary designations.
- **Action Step:** Set a calendar invite now for a January budget reset — you're building momentum, not just finishing a race.

Rolling & Life Event-Based Reminders

Throughout the year, adapt your strategy when major life changes occur:

- **Marriage, divorce, or a new child**
- **A move to a new district or state**
- **A significant pay increase, stipend, or bonus**
- **Transitioning into or out of the classroom**
- **Becoming eligible for pension or Social Security planning**

Quarterly Action Step: Every 3 months, review your savings progress, revisit goals, rebalance investments, and assess what's changed in your financial life.

Final Thought: Automate What You Can, Stay Engaged Where It Matters

Teachers are constantly pulled in different directions. The best way to stay on top of your finances? Automate your savings, your investments, and your calendar alerts — and reserve your energy for making the big-picture decisions with confidence.

Financial literacy becomes financial leadership when you apply it consistently.

Discipline + structure = financial peace. And peace is the reward you've earned.

Questions to Ask Before Hiring a Financial Professional

The right financial team can help you go from paycheck-to-paycheck to retirement-ready. Whether you're early in your career or preparing to retire after decades in the classroom, your choice of advisor matters. You don't need someone who just sells products — you need someone who listens, teaches, and guides with clarity and integrity.

Below are the essential questions you should ask before hiring a financial advisor, CPA, estate planning attorney, or any other professional who will help shape your financial future.

Questions to Ask a Financial Advisor

1. Are you a fiduciary 100% of the time?
2. Do you have experience working with educators, school employees, or public sector professionals?
3. How do you get paid — are you fee-only, fee-based, or do you earn commissions from selling products?
4. Can you help me make the most of my 403(b), 457, or pension options?
5. Will you help me understand how to coordinate my retirement income streams (pension, Social Security, IRAs, etc.)?
6. Do you help clients set financial goals like paying off student loans, buying a home, or saving for children's education?
7. Will you coordinate with my CPA, insurance agent, or estate attorney to ensure my full plan works together?
8. How do you choose investments — and how will you explain them in a

way I can actually understand?

9. Do you offer help with budgeting, debt payoff plans, and managing lifestyle changes like marriage or having kids?
10. How often will we meet, and how will you measure progress toward my financial goals?

Questions to Ask a CPA (Certified Public Accountant)

1. Do you have experience working with educators, government employees, or clients who have pension income?
2. Will you provide year-round tax planning, or just prepare my return at the end of the year?
3. Can you help me understand my educator-specific deductions (e.g., classroom supplies, union dues)?
4. Do you stay current on changes to retirement contribution limits and educator tax breaks?
5. Can you help me plan for retirement taxes, including how to withdraw from my pension and IRAs in a tax-efficient way?
6. Will you represent me in case of an audit?
7. How do you charge — flat fee, hourly, or percentage of assets — and what's included?
8. Will you work with my financial advisor to create a tax-smart retirement withdrawal strategy?

Questions to Ask an Estate Planning Attorney

1. Do you regularly work with middle-income families, teachers, or public service professionals?
2. What estate planning documents do I need — will, living trust, power of attorney, healthcare directive?
3. Can you help ensure my pension, retirement accounts, and insurance beneficiaries are aligned with my wishes?
4. Should I consider a trust to help my children or spouse avoid probate?

5. How often should I update my estate plan, and will you remind me when laws or life events change?
6. How do you charge for your services, and will I know the cost upfront?

Questions to Ask an Insurance Advisor

1. Are you an independent agent or do you only sell policies from one company?
2. Can you review my current life, auto, home, and disability coverage to make sure I'm properly protected?
3. Do I need life insurance beyond what the school district provides?
4. Can you help me compare term vs. whole life insurance?
5. What are the gaps in most teachers' insurance coverage that I might be overlooking?

Questions to Ask a Real Estate Professional

1. Do you understand the income patterns of teachers and how that impacts loan pre-approvals?
2. Can you help me understand how much house I can afford while still saving for retirement?
3. What first-time homebuyer programs or educator discounts are available in my state or district?
4. Will you help me think long-term — including resale value, commute, and school district quality?

Questions to Ask a Career Coach or Pension Counselor

1. Can you walk me through how my pension works — when I'm eligible, how it's calculated, and what options I have?
2. What happens to my pension if I leave teaching or move to a different state?
3. Can you help me understand early retirement options and what

tradeoffs I should consider?

4. Will you help me map out a "second-act" career plan after I retire from the classroom?

Final Thought: Build a Team That Honors Your Purpose

As a teacher, you've given your life to helping others succeed. Now it's your turn to be supported. The professionals you hire should educate you, empower you, and collaborate with each other. They should understand that you're not just building wealth — you're building a future with purpose.

And while this guide is educational, if you ever feel like you need more support, I'd be honored to help. My name is Pat Brown, MBA — a financial literacy advocate and wealth manager who works with many teachers just like you. Your financial plan should reflect your values, your goals, and your worth.

You've spent a career giving to others — now let's make sure your money gives back to you.

About the Author

Pat Brown, MBA, is a former Division I football player turned financial educator and trusted advisor who has spent more than two decades helping individuals, families, and communities build wealth with purpose. His journey—from student-athlete to respected wealth manager—has been shaped by one core belief: *financial literacy is the foundation for freedom, stability, and legacy.*

Raised in a household where money wasn't openly discussed, Pat knows firsthand how a lack of financial education can limit even the most promising futures. That early experience ignited his lifelong mission: to empower others—especially those in service-oriented professions—with the tools and confidence to take control of their financial lives.

After earning his MBA, Pat built a successful career in financial planning, investment strategy, and insurance. Over the years, he founded a series of financial literacy platforms to serve communities that are often overlooked or underserved. His projects include:

- *Financial Literacy for NIL*
- *Financial Literacy for Student Athletes*
- *Financial Literacy for the Culture*
- *Financial Literacy for College Coaches*
- *Financial Literacy for Parents of Student Athletes*
- *Financial Literacy for Doctors, Dentists, Attorneys, Pharmacists, Engineers, First Responders, and Expats*

Now, through *Financial Literacy for Teachers*, Pat brings that same passion to the people who shape futures every day—educators. Teachers are the backbone of our communities, yet many are left to navigate complex financial decisions with little guidance. From understanding pensions and managing student loans to budgeting on modest salaries and preparing for retirement, Pat's approach is designed to meet teachers where they are and guide them forward with clarity and compassion.

Pat's financial advice is practical, culturally aware, and built on real-world experience—not jargon or hype. Whether you're a first-year teacher trying to balance your budget or a veteran educator planning your exit from the classroom, this book will help you make smarter decisions about your money, your future, and your legacy.

In addition to his financial work, Pat serves as a Trustee on the Board of Lawrence Memorial Hospital (LMH) and sits on several nonprofit and civic boards focused on education, healthcare, and family support. He regularly speaks at conferences, churches, and community events—translating complex financial topics into conversations that inspire action.

Above all, Pat is a husband, father, and lifelong learner who believes teachers deserve more than thanks—they deserve financial empowerment. His mission is simple: *to make sure the people who spend their lives educating others finally get the education they deserve—about money, wealth, and freedom.*

Final Word

Need Help? Start Here

Financial Literacy for Teachers exists because we believe educators deserve more than gratitude—they deserve financial empowerment. You spend your career teaching others. Now it's time to make sure you're equipped to teach, protect, and elevate your own financial future.

This book is here to help you turn financial knowledge into financial action. Whether you're trying to make your salary stretch, understand your pension, plan for a future outside the classroom, or simply get more confident with money—this is your playbook. Not a rulebook, not a textbook—just a real-world, practical guide to help you make better decisions with the income and benefits you've worked hard to earn.

But let's be clear: success doesn't come from wishful thinking. It comes from structure, discipline, and small, consistent steps taken with purpose. You don't need to be an expert in every area of finance. You just need to know when to ask questions, when to seek help, and how to keep moving forward.

Use This Book Actively—Not Passively

Come back to it often. Highlight what resonates. Share sections with your spouse, your colleagues, your kids. Let it challenge you to think differently about money—not as a source of stress or scarcity, but as a tool to create security, freedom, and options for the life you want.

Not Sure Where to Start? Let's Talk

If you feel stuck or overwhelmed—or if you want personal guidance tailored to your situation—reach out. Whether you're just getting started or navigating more complex decisions (like managing student loans, pensions, side income, or preparing for retirement), you don't have to figure it all out alone.

Pat Brown, MBA

Financial Literacy Advocate | Wealth Advisor | Former Division I Athlete

Advisor to educators, student-athletes, professionals, and families across the country

Website: www.financialliteracyforteachers.com

Email: info@financialliteracyforteachers.com

LinkedIn: linkedin.com/in/patrickbrownmba

Want More Tools and Tips?

Sign up at www.financialliteracyforteachers.com for practical advice, monthly checklists, and easy-to-follow strategies designed specifically for educators. No jargon. No fluff. Just real help for real people.

Final Word: You Deserve Financial Peace

This isn't just about money. It's about freedom. Confidence. Options. Legacy. Whether you're 25 or 65, it's not too late to take control of your financial life. And it's never too early to build a future you're proud of.

So start where you are. Use what you have. Do what you can.

And remember—you teach others every day. Let this be the moment you give yourself the education you deserve.

Made in the USA
Monee, IL
04 November 2026

67387595R00125